Conflict

Resolution

How to Thoughtfully Handle
Difficult Situations

*(How Mindful Communication Supports Growth
Through Conflict)*

Kevin Bradford

Published By **Andrew Zen**

Kevin Bradford

All Rights Reserved

Conflict Resolution: How to Thoughtfully Handle Difficult Situations (How Mindful Communication Supports Growth Through Conflict)

ISBN   978-1-77485-843-1

No part of this guidebook shall be reproduced in any form without permission in writing from the publisher except in the case of brief quotations embodied in critical articles or reviews.

Legal & Disclaimer

The information contained in this ebook is not designed to replace or take the place of any form of medicine or professional medical advice. The information in this ebook has been provided for educational & entertainment purposes only.

The information contained in this book has been compiled from sources deemed reliable, and it is accurate to the best of the Author's knowledge; however, the Author cannot guarantee its accuracy and validity and cannot be held liable for any errors or omissions. Changes are periodically made to this book. You must consult your doctor or get professional medical advice before using any of the suggested remedies, techniques, or information in this book.

Upon using the information contained in this book, you agree to hold harmless the Author from and against any damages, costs, and expenses, including any legal fees potentially resulting from the application of any of the information provided by this guide. This disclaimer applies to any damages or injury caused by the use and application, whether directly or indirectly, of any advice or information presented, whether for breach of contract, tort, negligence, personal injury, criminal intent, or under any other cause of action.

You agree to accept all risks of using the information presented inside this book. You need to consult a professional medical practitioner in order to ensure you are both able and healthy enough to participate in this program.

TABLE OF CONTENTS

Introduction

When people hear the term "conflict" they are likely to see an over-exaggerated representation of it. It is believed that conflict takes the form of a violent or physical confrontation among groups (i.e. conflict or riots). The idea is that it's something that occurs only in certain areas of society, for instance political conflicts or among different ethnic groups. However, the reality is that conflicts are often triggered by tiny, unimportant issues and, most of the time it's not even intentional. Actually, the majority of conflicts are caused by errors, mistakes, or even miscommunication. However, conflict is everywhere and can take many different forms. In a world that is home to thousands of people each with their own experiences, opinions and desires to take care of it's difficult for everybody to reach a consensus. It's inevitable to have conflict.

Because it's impossible to completely avoid conflict So the best solution is to be able to manage it the best manner possible by learning the skills needed to settle conflicts quickly and efficiently. Without these capabilities, conflict can only get worse and grow and cause more issues to the increasing number of people in the conflict.

Let's face it, the resolution of conflicts isn't always simple. If it was simple and everyone could do it, then everybody would be able to do it and we wouldn't have to deal with the kind of harm it can cause to an individual, a business or an institution, or even a nation or continent.

Yet, once established, conflict resolution is an essential skill to possess. This book will be focused on conflict resolution within the workplace. Conflict with coworkers or with other office workers isn't just harmful to the individuals who are directly affected, but also has a negative impact on the company in general, manifested by a hostile work environment and a decline in productivity. There is good news, with a better understanding and a bit of strategy workplace conflicts is more easily prevented and solved. In this guide I'll teach you how to manage conflicts and reach mutually acceptable solutions that are which are agreeable for everyone. Additionally, you'll be taught how to create a conflict-free workplace to avoid conflicts before they even have the chance to escalate. If you're eager to make the first step toward making your workplace a more peaceful and efficient workplace, we can begin!

Chapter 1: Is About Conflict In The

Workplace

There's probably no better place to allow conflict to be brewed and felt more than in the workplace. Contrary to other social gatherings where people gather on the basis of something they have in common, workplaces like the workplace comprise of individuals who must be present regardless of their divergences. More often than not employees must get along with one another in order to achieve their objectives.

To be efficient the workplace, as well as its workers, must operate together. Any action that causes disruption or possibly disrupt any relationship at work could cause damage to the entire system. In our lives, we've had to work with people we would rather not work with and it can affect various aspects of our lives. The bosses may become less objective and employees may become distracted and colleagues can become less co-operative. This isn't always positive.

It's just Work. What's the point?

It is a common belief the resolution of conflicts is the sole responsibility of the human resources or someone in an executive position. It's not always the truth.

Although it's natural for the top officials to be the ones to decide on how conflicts are resolved however, anyone who works in the same space must be aware. You don't need to be an active participant of the conflict to realize that problems can be affecting you.

Imagine sitting at your desk and observing tension between two coworkers. It's not necessary to be aware of their names - they could be from another department altogether. It's enough to come across them in their situation. It doesn't matter if you're conscious of it and not kind of thing can affect your health as well.

It can get more severe. Take a look at the following:

Conflicts can cause a lot of stress that is not needed. They divert people's attention away from the things they should be focusing on instead. The distraction can be even more potent when tensions aren't obvious since the parties affected aren't able to vent their frustrations.

Conflicts in work groups cause them to disintegrate. The ability to work in teams is usually required in the workplace. Misunderstandings between the ranks could impact the entire group. This can make the team less productive, or truly damaging.

Conflicts put a huge stress on resources. It doesn't matter if we're talking about resources of the company or employees themselves and whether they're tangible resources such as capital, or intangible ones like energy and time Conflicts are simply an unnecessary use of many things. Employees could leave in the event that the stress becomes too much which can happen at the most inconvenient situations.

Conflicts also spread into the workplace. When they become heated the parties take the matter seriously and the families and friends of these employees begin to realize the extent of the damage their work has taken on them.

Therefore, whether you're a supervisor who mediates the conflict , or a casual observer who observes the gossip in the office, you're equally a participant in the resolution of conflicts as anyone else and not just because you have an immediate stake in the current conflict and, more importantly, because you, along with everyone else is interested in creating a peaceful work setting.

Furthermore the resolution of conflicts is a collaborative initiative. Because resolving conflicts and preventing them require a process and procedure, it is important for everyone who participates in the system is aware of the way things are conducted.

The resolution of conflicts, therefore, is something that everyone needs to learn to be able to do. This will ensure that understanding of grievance machines as well as preventive measures as well as other methods specifically designed to prevent workplace conflicts are maintained and accessible to all. The old saying goes, is the power of knowledge.

Beyond resolving conflict, this guide will explore the creation of a workplace that can resolve conflict when they do occur. This is a reference to:

• Understanding the characteristics of a resilient conflict-free workplace is like

Knowing the most the most common kinds of conflicts and being able to handle these conflicts

* Establishing a process to address conflicts as they occur

Do's and Don'ts to avoid during conflict.

This guide will use general principles of conflict resolution and apply them to workplace situations in the hope that it can help all parties who are interested in the creation of a peaceful and non-conflicting environment.

Chapter 2: Building An Environment

That Is Resilient To Conflict

Visualization is the initial step in creating an environment that is tolerant of conflict. You must know the way your workplace must look like in order capable of resolving any conflicts that could occur.

Workplaces that are resilient to conflict begin with Relations and Communication

The first and most important thing is that an environment that is conflict-free is always focused upon improving communication as well as creating relationships. This is due to the obvious reason that conflicts originate due to the absence of these two essential elements. Inability to communicate effectively, while more obvious conflicts are a result of a lack in respect for each other.

You would like your workplace to allow for the development of these two elements. Failure to grasp this at the beginning can cause the failure of the system for resolving conflicts from the beginning.

Workplaces that can withstand conflict are prepared for all phases of conflict

There are three phases of conflict, as illustrated by a very simple timeline: prior to when they occur when they occur, at times they're likely to happen and the time they occur.

A peaceful work environment should make it a priority to plan for all of these scenarios so that everyone is aware of what they need to do when the situation arises. In the ideal scenario, you'll want to avoid any conflicts - there's no use in waiting for things to escalate before you do anything about them. However, since these conflicts are likely to escalate due to a variety of reasons, everyone should be aware of what level of conflict they're in and what they should do in that particular moment.

This covers the systematic and logistical aspect of conflict-resolution (i.e. which direction to take and whom to contact in the event of an escalated conflict).

Being caught unaware as the conflict escalates could cause people to be in a position similar to being unprepared. It will, in turn it will lead to failure.

The methods for resolving conflicts differ between institutions, however the steps are generally the same

* The prevention stage is what most companies must focus their attention. The prevention of conflicts is the most cost-effective way to ensure the workplace is a place that is not prone to conflict. This is the reason why the company adopts measures to improve relationships between coworkers and also make sure that everyone is aware of the boundaries of their workplace through accurate communication and information.

The collaborative stage is when workers collaborate with one on a project that could be either short - or long-term. This is where the actions and decisions of all parties must be monitored to ensure that they do not cause conflict. It is also the time when those who may cause conflict are addressed to prevent any conflict from occurring. In this case, whether or not conflict will occur is contingent on the degree of cooperation between all parties.

The resolution phase begins at the point that disagreements develop between parties until the point that their disputes are settled. This typically will require that an official intervention via formal or informal procedures. This could be the last stage of a conflict , and the stage at which it needs to be resolved if irreparable harm to everyone at the workplace needs to be avoided.

Organizations with a strong resilience to conflict are context sensitive

Many workplaces are guilty of creating specific protocols and procedures to make them. However, when employees begin to use these features, it's like nothing is happening. Management implements these policies to impress and not to actually help its employees.

Each workplace is unique and has its own set of demands. Therefore, the services offered must be tailored to meet the requirements of each workplace. the system for conflict resolution is not any different. What is considered to be within acceptable norms in one workplace may not be acceptable from one workplace to another. This is also true when it comes to policy-making (i.e. certain offices require the wearing of uniforms whereas other offices are more relaxed with the uniform code). What is acceptable practice or legally binding regulation will vary from office to office.

The resolution of conflicts must be sensitive at an individual and a micro level. This means that management must be clear about the acceptable behavior standards for employees, but simultaneously remain alert to any exceptions.

Conflict-resistant workplaces are in compliance with Regulations

When rules are established and enforced, they must be adhered to. Inability to implement them effectively and in a fair way will result in people losing faith in the system, resulting in its demise and possibly a long-term inability to address the issues.

The concept of a conflict resilient workplace is dependent on the enforcer's capacity to enforce these rules but it will require some cooperation of employees.

No matter how many people are cooperating the system that's been created to settle complaints and to prevent conflict must be allowed to follow the course it wants to in every instances.

Conflict-resilient workplaces are evolving

Since no system will ever be 100% perfect, it's vital to recognize that the model for conflict resolution for any workplace is likely to remain a work-in-progress. The reason for this is that the effectiveness of the model depends by its ability to tackle many different problems. Each time a conflict is resolved successfully or not, it's crucial for everyone to examine the overall effectiveness of the model as in the current case.

A model for conflict resolution that is evolving will also be able identify the kind of issues that it must address by asking questions such as:

1. What's the root cause of the issue? Was it preventable?

If the problem grew was there any ways that could be taken to stop it earlier?

What was the effect of the conflict on the workplace?

1. What's the outcome implemented? Was it the right one considering the circumstances?

These types of questions and more aid the management in understanding the root cause and the severity of the issues and better prepare to tackle issues in the near future. There will certainly be areas of improvement especially in the beginning.

Ideally, you'll strive to create an environment that encourages the mentioned values as far as the resolution of conflicts is involved. The way you can attain these goals will be contingent on your particular situation, however, this guide will help you achieve your goals.

Chapter 3: Evolving Conflict

Resolution Model

Since conflict resolution models at work are still in development it is crucial to understand the various ways to build this specific model. Seven steps to complete:

1. Establishing representation

2. Evaluating status quo

3. Recognizing areas to improve

4. Making plans of actions

5. Implementation plans are being developed.

6. Implementation

7. Post implementation evaluation

Each step is a distinct procedure that requires you to meet short-term objectives to reach the ultimate goal of establishing the system to stop and resolve conflicts.

Step 1: Establishing Representation. Conflict can be avoided and solved through effective communication and tolerance among different parties with different perspectives and preferences. It is crucial that the team creating the process for conflict resolution comprises representatives from all possible parties (i.e. employees in the rank and file, managers and management). Eliminate a significant person and the process for resolving conflicts be affected. This could result in the failure of the system and could result in non-cooperation.

Note: How complicated the representative body is is dependent in the scale of the office. If you're in an office that is small It's possible that one person could be assigned to the entire job. It's crucial that all requirements are considered in the process.

Step 2: Assessing the Status Quo. Most often it's not necessary to start from scratch when trying to create an effective system for resolving conflicts. Even without one who have been in the field for a long time without knowing it, have a way of resolving conflicts, and it's not recognized and systematically implemented. Perhaps your workplace already has someone to are able to call when they have an issue, or your coworkers have a system to solve a stalemate when it comes to decision-making.

Taking advantage of what people working in the workplace are comfortable with can encourage cooperation in resolving disputes.

If there's no known method for solving conflicts, you can conduct an investigation of the culture of conflict in the workplace.

Which is your most frequent problem that the workplace frequently encounters?

Are there any complaints about unsatisfaction?

What are the issues getting addressed any point?

In this stage in this step, the aim of the group is to come up with a list of suggestions that must be addressed. That's where, by applying the concepts mentioned in the previous section, you'll develop a resiliency to conflict that is specific in your company.

TIP: Always be neutral when evaluating the status in the present. Always search for evidence to support the existence of issues that might otherwise be overstated or exaggerated since you'll want to tackle the real issues.

Third Step: Finding the Areas to improve. This is a step that sounds similar to the first since they both go hand-in-hand. Once you have established the recommended actions then you must determine the way in which these recommendations are directed toward the goals in the work environment. In this stage you will be able to:

* Create a checklist of these areas to improve

* Discuss which areas are most important to prioritize.

* Determine who is accountable for the improvement aspect within the system

Step 4: Develop Courses of Action. There are numerous methods to accomplish a single objective This step is focused on choosing the best path to pursue. There is always a option that is superior to all other. Take into consideration the following aspects in determining the best option:

* Which one is the most appropriate to meet the requirements of all participants?

* Which method is the most efficient in terms of cost (i.e. costs less but provides the same end outcome)

* Which one is the easiest to sustain over the long run?

TIP: Try creating an inventory of all possible options in one column, and then write down the pros and cons of each option. This will help break the links between seemingly equal choices.

Step 5: Design Implementation Plans. After discussions have been concluded and all options have been approved then it's time to outline the steps to implement these actions. It is important to determine the following aspects:

1. The person or people tasked with carry out the plan

2. Timeline for the job that includes milestones and deadlines

3. Working budget

4. Consultation: Who are the individuals whose collaboration is required?

Be sure to make allowances for these specifics. There are times when plans don't go as planned. Some timelines could be delayed or cost increased. Be prepared to be prepared for unexpected.

Step 6 The implementation. This step is pretty straightforward. Make certain that anyone responsible to carry out the changes adheres to the guidelines as closely as is possible.

Step 7 Step 7: Post Implementation Assessment. Consider it as an after-test the context of Step 2. Simply evaluate the post-implementation situation by asking the following questions:

* Did the goals you set met?

* Were the identified issues and areas for improvement addressed or addressed?

What were the main difficulties encountered in the course of the project? What was the solution?

* What can the new system be developed?

The cycle begins again. For as long as the model for conflict resolution is in operation it will always have the need for improvement. This will require additional plan and implementation when time passes along.

Chapter 4: The Most Common Types

Of Conflict In The Workplace

There are various types of workplace conflicts, however there are general categories. These classifications aren't exhaustive, since the nature of conflicts varies depending on the situation. You might have experienced or witnessed them in some way or other way.

Discrimination

Although the workplace is governed by rank but the equality of all employees from the same rank should be a mandatory requirement. Yet, there are some who are unjustly classified at work, mostly because of their ethnicity or gender. It can take many forms like:

* Being assigned smaller or larger parts of a group task, and where everyone has to contribute equally;

* Being either directly or indirectly exclusion by coworkers from work-related activities within the the workplace or

* Receiving less benefits as compared to other workers who perform the same work.

Discrimination cases in the workplace are a long and sometimes endless list because there are numerous ways to discriminate against an individual unfairly. Sometimes, they are difficult to identify, or because the individual doesn't realize that they are being discriminated against, or simply accepts the treatment or doesn't have an avenue to express their issue.

There are occasions of discrimination which escalate to mediation, the majority conflicts of this kind should be resolved using preventive actions. In most cases, the establishment should not look outside of the laws that are within their area of jurisdiction to identify what constitutes as discriminatory. Furthermore, the company's management can establish specific guidelines for promoting equality of treatment for all employees in the workplace.

Conflicts in Leadership

Sometimes, leaders aren't able to make the best decisions. When working in a group it is expected that subordinates raise a concern about the superior's judgement or the authority of the leader.

The thing that makes this type of conflict difficult is the fact that in some instances, the subordinate may be right in pointing out the leader's error. One hand, the it is the norm that the leader be the ultimate judge. On the otherhand, the leader might make a mistake that could lead to the demise of the whole team.

There must be a clear definition of who is entitled to make the decisions that will stop such situations from spiralling out of control. Management must be mindful that they do not ignore the concerns of their subordinates since they also have a stake in ensuring the team is successful in any initiatives it's tackling.

Large-scale leadership conflicts can occur between the majority of workers as well as the people on the boards or director of the business. This is when strike or lockouts could occur.

Whatever the size regardless of size, there's usually formal and informal mechanisms to assist parties in negotiating their differences. Most of the time, these problems can be solved through the process of negotiating an agreement between the two parties.

Personal Conflicts

Although bosses might prefer to keep out of the lives of their employees in the outside world Employees have a way of bringing their own personal issues to the workplace. It's true that this is a variety of ways and requires two basic types of strategies.

The first step is to determine If the conflict between coworkers is a result of an incident in your workplace (i.e. workplace talk or even bullying) It is important to intervene and correct the issue since the incident is directly linked to work.

If the dispute originates from an issue which has nothing to do with work It is usually best for management to take a step back and take action when the tension is already affecting other employees in the workplace. Companies must be cautious not to give authority beyond the workplace.

Similar to most personal conflicts these conflicts can be resolved with the proper mediation of a person whom both parties can trust. Most of the time the misunderstandings can be resolved in a calm manner. In the event of disagreements that are irreconcilable coworkers must at the very least be instructed to put their differences aside while working.

Conflicts of Responsibility

If there is a problem at work, confusion can ensue and conflicts arise. Problems regarding who was responsible to be doing what, and who was responsible for what begin to surface. People begin playing blame games and no one is willing to accept responsibility for any bad thing that occurs, fearing the consequences.

Sometimes, coworkers don't handle criticisms well even from superior officials, and this can result in personal conflicts or even discrimination.

Conflicts of this kind arise due to an overall misallocation or failure to allocate of responsibility or workload. This is only possible to resolve them by establishing clear boundaries of responsibility among colleagues and laying the foundation for standards that everyone has to follow.

There are a myriad of types of workplace conflicts however, one thing they all share is the fact that they are avoided or resolved by a system of conflict resolution.

Chapter 5: Conflict Resolution From

An Individual Perspective

If or not there's any conflict resolution system in the place you work, be prepared that conflicts will arise and you'll have to be aware of how to act in these situations to end the conflict or, at minimum, to not make the situation more difficult. Here are some suggestions to consider:

Establish clear guidelines for conduct. A lot of personal conflicts occur because people believe the actions they're taking are acceptable. When they know what everyone in the workplace thinks is acceptable and unacceptable behaviour individuals are better equipped to stay within the rules, greatly lessening the likelihood of conflict.

A guidelines for conduct can be useful to improve interpersonal relations with coworkers, as well as for the work ethic of employees.

Listen. The majority of conflict stems because people aren't able to convey their opinions. If people are not heard or their needs aren't satisfied, they get angry and may escalate the issue to a higher management level, when it could have been addressed in a matter of minutes.

Your colleagues and your boss are also people and have their own demands. While management may not be able to resolve the individual issues of each worker but it can strive to create an environment that allows for individual issues are considered, and are discussed.

Decide which conflicts to confront and which ones to avoid. The type of dispute confronting a problem head-on can ease tension or cause more harm. The issue is, how do you know what is the right one? There are several tests you can take to aid in making that decision.

The first test is known as"the "right individual test". Check if you're in a position to tackle the issue. If someone who works for you raises an issue about a colleague It is best to refer them to the appropriate person who is able to handle the complaints. If you're the project director of a group and one member of your team members has an issue, ensure you take care of it as it's your responsibility.

Sometimes, we find ourselves compelled to become involved in other people's problems, but placing your fingers in areas where you shouldn't is only going to cause conflict to escalate.

Another test known as the "what's going on for me" test. Be aware that conflict does not always directly impact the work environment. Certain coworkers might not be each other's eyes, but their differences are at most evident. If you're not sure that the dispute between two people could have an impact on the workplace, it's best not to pay the issue any attention. If the issue has a negative impact on you or your colleagues in any way that is significant it might be time to take action.

The final test is called"worth" test "worth" check. Simply ask yourself: Is being involved in the situation worth the effort?

Sometimes, people get involved in conflicts because of a small reason The best way to handle it is to take the higher way and relax. There is no need to engage in conflict just to get it done. The process of resolving conflicts can help relieve the stress of conflict and not cause more stress.

These guidelines are for anyone who has to deal with an issue of conflict at work - whether the leader, member, manager or employee.

Chapter 6: What To Do To Take

Here are some tips that you should not do caught in the middle of a conflict.

Do not be scared of conflict. You must be aware that conflict is a natural part of life The worst spot to be in is the dark. Don't be surprised because you believed that everything would be in order each day.

When you're faced with any situation, be aware that you've got a company that can help you. Yes, it can be stressful however, giving into the fear can just make your judgement worse.

If you view the resolution of conflicts as only a part of the job, you'll be in a position to accept it as a part of your daily responsibilities by allowing yourself to be in charge.

Do not let your emotions influence your judgement. It is important not to be swept away. Most of the time the way you react to the possibility of conflict will determine whether or not there's going to be conflict start with. Therefore, if something frightens you or angers you Make it a routine to not speak up then look away, and consider what you'll be saying the next time.

Don't be a partisan. Whatever you think about it, no matter how you may be in agreement with one side in a conflict it is important to remain neutral. This can be the best way to be sure that both parties respect your guidance when they present the issue up to you.

A split will only make one person feel marginalized which can cause the other to be more aggressive or to feel resentful and ostracized. Whatever the case, the conflict will eventually grow.

When you take neutrality that is neutral, both parties will be more inclined to accept your arguments than should they believe that you were untruthful. It's crucial to always assure everyone that you've got your best interests in mind.

Don't put others at fault. There's a difference between knowing what caused the problem and then putting blame on other people. It is better to look at failure and success as shared by everyone, rather than a single person. So, it'll be more palatable and absorbed by the individual responsible for the fault.

In reality having an entire group of colleagues who acknowledge collective successes and failures creates an environment in which it's easy for individuals to admit their own mistakes.

If you do know the person responsible Don't fall for the reflex of finger-pointing. This doesn't do anything, other than to make things worse.

If, on the other hand, you realize that you're in the wrong then you should admit to it. People will be impressed by it.

Don't believe everyone outright. A common cause of conflict is the reaction of people to events that have no foundation (i.e. gossip, accusations). Although it is essential to have confidence in the people whom you interact with, it is important to treat any accusations or issues with a grain of salt. This will not only protect your integrity, but will also help you control your emotions prior to taking action in the event that it's genuine.

Do not get too involved in conflicts. This is especially important if the conflict is confined to work. Take your work off at home and do not allow it to bother you once you return home. This won't resolve the issue.

Also, you should learn to accept that there isn't anything in your hands. Sometimes, problems arise in the workplace because the people were not prepared for it. Certain people can be difficult to work with.

There are many conflicts that cannot be stopped or resolved completely. What you should do in these instances is to simply accept the things you cannot alter and then get back to your work.

Chapter 7: The High-Conflict Couple

Divorce

High-conflict divorce isn't the usual type of stress. You may be rushing to get your schedule in order, over time for a meeting being called to the office of your boss or having an oil leak--these could cause you to feel anxious and overwhelmed for a short time. However, high-conflict divorces is so painful and lasting that it can affect both your brain as well as your body.

Knowing the reaction that you might experience and knowing what to watch out for and learning new strategies to handle the emotional turmoil of divorce with high conflict can help you stay on the right track. Divorce is a difficult time for every person. The separation of the family unit, splitting up the property, and trying to navigate an "new normal" are not easy tasks even if the split is not acrimonious. If you're divorced from a high-conflict person, the term "stress" could not be enough to describe the emotions you're experiencing.

Trauma and chronic stress

Stress is beneficial. It encourages us to take care of ourselves and act. Our bodies are built to react to stress. When they sense danger, our bodies release stress hormones to prepare to fight or flee. Our muscles become tense as breathing speeds up and heart rate rises and digestive processes slow in order to give energy to other areas so that we are prepared to fight for our lives. If we're in constant and lasting stress, our hormone levels remain in a state of high. Our bodies aren't made to handle such a situation. In time the imbalance could cause damage to both physical and emotional well-being.

If we're in a relationship that is toxic or have a divorce that is high-conflict Our bodies could be conditioned to be in this state of alert which means that we're constantly in a state of alert. It's possible that you're trying to remain in your home, maintain the custody of your children or perhaps stay out of the prison or rehabilitation. Discord, dirty divorce techniques and constant anxiety could lead to emotional stress.

Common Reactions

Everyone is different when confronted by a crisis in their lives. The way you react will be influenced by many aspects, such as your health, personality as a child, your childhood, prior adult experiences, your experience in your relationship with others or in your marriage and the degree of conflict you're experiencing in your divorce.

It could be that you are experiencing:

* Feeling overwhelmed: Feeling as if you're overwhelmed and avoiding, procrastinating.

* Tiredness or fatigue You feel tired and sluggish. down, and the kind of fatigue that a decent night's sleep won't help.

* Depression or sadness A prolonged bout of crying and being shy and lack of interest.

* Anxiety, fear or anxiety attacks: Feeling more anxious than usual, getting anxious, easily agitated or worried excessively.

* Irritation or anger Anger or irritability: Having trouble dealing with anger, becoming angry at minor issues and easily annoyed, or complaining more often than normal.

* Ruminating or obsessing about Obsessed or ruminating: getting caught thinking negative thoughts and or thinking about the same thoughts repeatedly.

* Self-blame, guilt: Self-criticism, shame, guilt Feeling responsible in a way, feeling inadequate.

* Changes in appetite or weight eating either more or less food than normal suddenly losing weight or weight gain, a inability to eat.

* Migraines or headaches Experience migraines or headaches more frequently, with more intensity, or with a longer duration.

• Trouble sleeping or nightmares: Insomnia difficulty in staying asleep or wake up early and having dreams or nightmares.

* Muscle tension The tightness of your neck or shoulders tightness in your legs the jaw is clenched.

* Nausea, heartburn, or vomiting: Having trouble eating or drinking food nauseating, burning sensations in the chest or throat.

* Changes in bowel habits such as diarrhea or constipation, IBS.

Menstrual cycle: More or longer painful menstrual periods more frequent or less frequent menstrual periods.

* Bodyaches Pain and general discomfort.

These symptoms are all common. The majority of people experiencing divorce suffers from one of these at some point or different. It all depends on your personal situation and the level of conflict you're experiencing you might find you're experiencing difficulties. Be aware of your bodily reactions and the effect they could have on your daily life. You can ask a family member or counselor to watch for any changes they observe. Here are the more serious conditions to be aware of:

Depression

Depression is a very common disorder that can hinder your capacity to live life to the fullest. Many people struggle in depression even though they are feeling very down. Some may have difficulty to go to work or get up. Depression can be dangerous, but it is easily treated with therapies, coping techniques and medications. If not addressed it could cause the appearance of a downward spiral as well as the inability to figure out a way out.

Anxiety

A lot of people suffer from anxiety from time-to-time. If you are spending a lot of time worrying, even though there's no actual threat or the worry isn't in line with the circumstance, it may impact other aspects that you live. The signs of anxiety can include:

* A lot of anxiety or concern over a wide range of subjects

* The worry that you are trying to manage

* Reluctance

* Fatigue

* Having trouble concentrating or being completely blank

* Irritability

* Nausea, vomiting or diarrhea

PTS Disorder (PTSD)

It's normal to feel anxious, stressed or anxious after experiencing a traumatizing incident. A lot of people recover, however there are some who experience painful symptoms and memories relating to the incident. Genetics, personal history social support, genetics, and many other aspects can influence the likelihood of someone developing PTSD after a trauma.

The symptoms of PTSD could be akin to:

* Traumatic memories or disturbing nightmares.

* Don't talk about the event that was traumatic.

The negative thoughts that plague you, the difficulty in keeping close relationships, loss of interest in the activities you used to enjoy.

* Physical and emotional reaction change: feeling scared or startled easily; having trouble getting sleep or concentrating; anger

There are many emotions that can be experienced in divorce that is high conflict and sharing them with someone who is safe to share these feelings is crucial. There are three main reasons to pay the reactions you're experiencing and discover ways to handle and deal in a way that is appropriate:

* You aren't able to make the right choices when the nervous system isn't functioning properly Divorce is about choices. What should you do, how to bargain, when to settle and when to hold to your convictions. It's not wise to avoid the situation or to react in anger. It won't give the results you desire or what's most beneficial for your children's future or your own.

Inability to manage your emotions could be applied against your character: If you fail to function effectively because of the emotional state you are in Your spouse may be recording it. Social media posts or texts that are explosive postings could be used to depict you as a conflict-prone person. A simple thing as children mentioning that mom was tired to cook dinner last night may cause custody disputes.

* Other people can be affected when you fail to manage your emotions. When you're not feeling well and you're not feeling well, your children, coworkers or friends are also affected. While it is hard on you, your kids must be able to depend on your role as a parent that can provide stability and security rather than someone who adds on their load. Your employer needs to be confident in your ability to show up and complete your job efficiently. Friends and family members don't have the right to be the target of your rage or be able to evade your worries.

Your emotional health is vital. Maintaining a healthy emotional balance will help you to get through divorce, assist your children, and plan your most successful future. Don't forget what you're feeling or the way it affects your life. It's likely that you're not capable of changing your situation however, you can put steps and habits put in place to help be more comfortable while dealing with it.

When you go through a divorce with a high degree of conflict it is possible to be caught in what's often referred to as "stinking about":

* This is just so unfair.

* My children are likely to be adamant about me and completely messed up for ever.

* Nobody cares about what I've gone through.

* I'll never be able to see my kids again/pay my bills or feel comfortable again.

* I feel weak/I'm not enough strong.

This could be one of the most difficult times you'll experience. Thinking about negative thoughts could increase depression, hamper thinking and problem-solving abilities, and cause you to lose important social assistance. What can you do to stop the cycle when you feel stuck?

You can try repeating the mantra, or an affirmation to combat this negative thought:

* I'm still able to make the best choices for myself.

* I'm a wonderful parent and can be a loving parent to my children.

There are friends who care and love me.

* I'll have everything I want in my life - maybe not at the moment however, but very soon.

* I'm capable of doing difficult things. I've made it to this point and I'm going.

Self-talk can be used to overcome negative thoughts. Ask yourself questions like:

* Is this a feeling , or is it a fact?

Is this useful?

* Does this allow me to get what I'm looking for?

* Is this a hiccup or an accident?

* Is there a better way to view this?

Chapter 8: Couple Conflict

Resolution

The most pleasant relationships also have conflict and issues. This can lead to development in both personal and relationships when handled properly. A variety of skills can assist those trying to resolve disputes in a safe manner. Effective communication is among the most important skills that aids in the resolution of conflicts.

In relationships, issues or conflicts are a result of any situation, event or experience that has an impact on or is relevant to the parties involved. There are many of causes that cause conflicts, and some are related to financial issues or children, in-laws and children, personal issues like self-esteem and aspirations, beliefs, or preferences, or questions like the time spent together and time apart and power versus support, the power of affection and communication.

There are a myriad of causes of conflict however, they are generally based on people's basic needs which include intellectual, physical emotional, social and spiritual. The outcome will depend on how we handle and deal with the questions.

The majority of people are aware that we must communicate on the subject to solve conflict, but unproductive communications patterns often cause more anger and an increase in conflict. Take a look at the following communication issues:

Body Language/Voice Communication

The tone goes beyond the words we decide to use. Sometimes, we speak with our voice and body language more loudly than the words we use. Screaming out "I'm in no way angry" as an example is not the most convincing signal. If we convey a contradicting message in which our voice and body language are not consistent with our message, miscommunications, and sometimes anger, are the result.

To conquer this communication hurdle We must be aware of what communicates the body language we use and voice transmit to other people. Make sure to speak with calmness, maintain eye contact, smile when needed and maintain an relaxed, open posture.

Different styles of dressing

Each one of us has a particular manner of interacting, typically depending on the interactions we have with our family, our history and gender as well as other variables. As an example, when we're not to our spouse our appearance can be louder, social, or emotional. Although there is no proper or incorrect way to dress but our experiences generally result in expectations that aren't usually spoken about with others creating tension and miscommunication. For example, If we come from an extended family with a tendency to shout in order to be heard, we might believe that it's normal to talk loudly. If our friend was from a more tranquil family, they might be uncomfortable, or even scared of an elevated voice.

Discussion of our experiences and views can help us understand other people's expectations, and will help our partners understand our viewpoint. This knowledge can aid in solving problems.

Communication Obstacles to communication

Communication issues are created when two individuals communicate in a manner that no one feels heard. The research has identified four negative communication styles. They are often described as "the four horsemen of the Apocalypse,"" since if they are not controlled these communication styles can cause harm to relationships. Criticism, disdainand defensiveness and stonewalling are some of these types.

* Criticism can be used to attack someone's personality or character.

Although it's normal to be concerned about someone else's actions, it's different from criticizing them in a way that is personal. A case in point might consist of: "I felt worried when you didn't contact me to let me know that you'd be late for work." Criticism can be expressed in the same manner like "You're too unconsidered that you never contact me when you're likely to arrive late." Criticism is focused on specific behaviors while criticism is focused upon the motivations, character and motives the individual.

* Contempt communicates displeasure and disrespect through body language such as eye-rolling and calling names or sarcasm. It can also be portrayed as cutting remarks towards the other.

The natural tendency to defend yourself is often a response to criticism or disrespect by individuals, however, it also escalates the issue.

When we're defensive, it's easy to tend to not listen to the perspective of others and sever contact.

Stonewalling withdraws from discussion and refuses to take part to the conversation.

It's the adult equivalent to"silent therapy "silent treatment" used by children when they are upset. If you don't touch your skin, dispute resolution isn't likely.

Other examples of communication obstacles are:

* Order ("Quit making complaints!")

* A word of caution ("If you violate this then you'll regret it.")

* Counseling ("You shouldn't be acting like that.")

* Recommendation ("Wait at least a few years until you make a decision")

* Reading ("If you're doing this today and you don't become an adult who is responsible")

* Agreeing, but only to ensure peace ("I believe that you're correct")

Recognizing the obstacles and trying to communicate effectively will assist people overcome roadblocks.

Strategies for Resolving Conflict

* Make it easier to start One of the techniques to deal with communication issues requires a gentle beginning to the discussion by starting with the positive, expressing gratitude, pondering on issues by one at a time and taking responsibility for your thoughts and emotions. Also,

starting the conversation by using "I" rather than "You" can reduce negative feelings and promote positive interactions in the conversation with other people while explaining the problem. For example: "I want to stay more active in making financial decision" rather than "you do not involve my input in your financial decision-making."

* Receive and Make Repair Tentative: Another crucial capability for overcoming roadblocks in contact is to learn how to accept and make attempts to repair. Repairs are attempts to stop the possibility of a more hostile environment by having a break or trying to ease the situation. This is important since we are often under extreme physical and emotional tension when there is a disagreement that can hinder the ability of us to reason and think, which can lead to communication stumbling blocks. The ability to take a break from the conflict to relax (at minimum 20 minutes) can allow us to be better prepared to discuss the issue.

Speech and Listening Skills are crucial it is essential to have excellent listening and speaking skills to overcome communication barriers. There's a method for talking and listening that can help people communicate better. Each person takes turns to be the speaker and listener.

The Speaker Rules Cover:

* It is important to share thoughts or feelings and worries.

* Make use of the "I" expressions whenever you speak to communicate the thoughts or feelings clearly.

* Keep the statements brief of making sure that information doesn't overload the listener.

* Stop after each brief phrase so that the person listening is able to paraphrase what has been stated to make sure that he or she understands or repeat it in their own phrases. If the paraphrase isn't entirely correct, change the sentence gently to aid the listener in understanding.

The Rules of the Listener Include:

* Copy what the orator is saying. If the message is unclear, ask for clarification. Follow until the speaker confirms that the message was received.

* Do not disagree or express an your opinion on the message of the speaker. Just wait until you're the speaker and then treat them with respect.

* The listener must not talk or interrupt the speaker is speaking other than paraphrasing the speaker.

Chapter 9: Couple Conflict

Resolution Strategies

Slashing doors, angry words silence, slamming doors, and many other harmful behaviors are the normal when two individuals in a relationship are always fighting. Verbal abuse can be as harmful as physical violence So don't fool yourself that because you're fighting only verbally this means that you're not harming each other. Human beings are emotionally wired. However, it is those we love the most who cause us the most harm. In every relationship, conflict is bound to occur.

If two people with distinct backgrounds and differing belief systems meet, there are likely to encounter situations where you'll disagree. The issue with relationships isn't that there's conflict, but how the conflict is resolved. If you are unable to resolve disagreements without screaming match or a sarcastic attitude towards each other, you've got unhealthy ways of dealing with conflicts.

It is important to approach disagreements to settle the issue and not force your opinions on another. Absolutes such as "never" as well as "always" could make you blind and make it difficult to make sound choices. Be careful not to make decisions when you are angered. Remain away to the issue until you are relaxed enough to be able to engage in conversation.

Victory in The Battle to Lose the War

Do you want to engage in two hours of argument about who didn't get rid of the garbage? It's not uncommon to see couples engaged in frenzied arguments over the smallest of things. It becomes a routine over time and you begin to realize that the occasions that you're in harmony with your partner diminish every day. It is therefore crucial to be aware of how to choose your conflicts.

While you're not going to wish to allow your partner get all over you to the point of getting agitated over small issues can be self-defeating. Being a victim of a persistent partner can drain you emotionally and make the other person leave. There's a reason people leave work early and head straight for the bar, instead of heading home to their loved ones. There's nothing more important than peace of mind and when you can't achieve it at home, you begin to look elsewhere for it.

Most people think that the act of nagging can be interpreted as criticism. It instantly puts the person in a defensive position. The person you are talking to will likely be able to tune you out as soon as you begin to talk in the event that they've grown accustomed to your constant nagging. Gradually, they begin to hate them because they feel like they are being personally attacked.

You stand a higher chance of success if you communicate with each other in a casual and casual manner. Avoid the temptation of making a fuss about them the moment they enter the door. Find the best moment to discuss problems, but make sure that your partner is at ease and open to discussion. Avoid causing further conflict and disagreements within your relationship by understanding how to be able to disagree without hurting your partner.

Living in Harmony

Do's

It's fine to have a disagreement. Every conflict doesn't have to be resolved by both parties reaching the same understanding. For certain issues it is necessary to accept different opinions.

* Keep personal attacks out of disagreements. Talk about the issues, not the person. Avoid bringing on your partner's shortcomings to make them feel uneasy of their own abilities or to pressure you into cajoling your.

* Remain in disagreement with the present, and resist the urge to dig up old problems and mistakes from the past.

* Stop combining all of your problems and then integrating them into one large

problem. Address issues as they pop up and figure out solutions for each one, don't accumulate all of your complaints to be used later on as an argument against your spouse.

• Take responsibility for your role to the issue. It takes two people to dance, and both of you have contributed to the majority of the conflicts within your relationship. If you admit to what you could have committed a mistake, you inspire the other to admit their mistakes. This helps you resolve and get over the issue. Being stubbornly steadfast in your position even when you are aware that you're not right, does not solve disagreements.

* Mind your language. Avoid using derogatory words or insults to prove an argument. Make sure the conversation is civil and refrain from causing anger. The more you criticize your opponent, the more shut off they are, and the less likely to resolve your disagreement.

Create a secure space in which you can relax without having to talk about the issue. It could be your bedroom, or any other space you feel is needed to be protected from conflict. This can take some of the stress away and give you a secure space to process your emotions.

Choose the time when you will be able to discuss the problem and bring it to an end. You don't want to revisit the same question for days at a time. Put aside the issue and decide to come to a consensus at the end of the time , and then let it go. It could be as long as an hour, 30 minutes, or even if you think you must discuss the issue and solve the issue.

Don'ts

* Don't try for victory by adhering with your position regardless of. If you think of conflict as a fight for supremacy, it'll be difficult to see anything solved.

* Don't think of your partner as a competitor. In all circumstances, remember that you're still in the partnership together and have to continue living together after the dispute has ended.

Don't be manipulative. Making threats, threats, and manipulation to achieve your goals can mean that the dispute cannot be solved. That means that you'll end up having the same argument you were trying to get out sooner or later.

* Don't commit a lie. Even if you're afraid of the consequences, you should do not be tempted to deceive or mislead your spouse. Be honest and open.

* Don't allow your emotions to get the best of your. Afraid or defensive behavior can hinder effective communication . If you are required to stop the conversation until you're at peace enough to be able to participate in a constructive manner.

* Don't make use of the past to hurt the person you are with or as a basis for your decision. Take care of the present issue without making assumptions based on previous experiences.

* Do not just agree to make it easier. Make yourself clear and refrain from saying "yes" just to please another person. If you are a regular of settling for getting

to know each other, you will always feel unhappy as you're trying to conceal your feelings.

The art of Compromise

It's not about giving an individual. It is a sign that you realize that you both have requirements and that the best approach to meet them is to meet in the middle.

A willingness to compromise is the ability to accept and respect the needs of the other person, without sacrificing your personal preferences. If you're in a relationship, but don't know what to do, the relationship is likely to be filled with tensions. Everyone likes their way, but if you've decided to be in a relationship with someone else, you must to realize that you are not the only option.

If you are willing to compromise as aspect of how you deal with disagreements within the relationship you build the security and trust in the relationship. Each partner is aware that when they may have different needs they will find an avenue to meet the needs of one another. This improves the harmony of your relationship, and increases your emotional bond.

To be willing to compromise within relationships, you have to be flexible and adaptable. You should be able to alter your viewpoint and look at the situation from the other's perspective.

Enhancing the Empathy of Your Partner

One of the best ways to get to know the other person is to walk from their perspective. This is about being sympathetic and allowing yourself to look beyond your own desires and feelings. Empathy is the feeling of the other person and observing things from their point of view.

You know where they're getting their information from when you build the empathy you have for your partner. This is vital in resolving conflict in your relationship. When you're closed to your partner the entire attention will be on you and your thoughts and that prevents you from being able to feel the emotions of the person you are experiencing.

Empathy boosts compassion and increases the bond of two persons. What could be more satisfying than feeling loved and feeling validated in the context of a relationship? Although empathy is a skill that most people acquire in their childhood, not all can use it effectively.

Here are some ideas to help you increase your empathy for your spouse:

Be present

If you're busy and oblivious, it is difficult to be aware of the emotions of your partner. Be active with your partner as instead of performing the routine. Turn off your cell phone or other electronic devices while you're spending time with your spouse. This will help you be present in the moment and increases your understanding of one another.

Change roles

If you're having trouble understanding the needs of your partner you should try changing roles. You could even play the role of to aid you. If you are able to put yourself in the shoes of another you gain a better understanding of what they're dealing with and how it feels to be their situation. It's easy to be selfish because you don't know what your spouse is going through. When you are in their position you will gain important insight into their moods and their needs.

Don't be a judge

Even if you don't like your co-worker Be respectful and respectful in your disagreement. Avoid being judgemental or critical. Keep in mind that everyone has had experiences that have affected their perspective on things. Don't think that your viewpoint is superior. Everyone has the right to their own needs. The best you can do is to be flexible and open.

Stop thinking

It's easy to misunderstand people in the assumption that we understand their feelings or what they want. Ask questions and encourage your companion to be open with you to ensure that you are able to comprehend what they are in need of. Sometimes just having a lengthy dialogue with your spouse will alter the way you view them, and improve your ability to feel the emotions they're experiencing. We've said it before there is nothing better than effective communication in the course of a relationship.

Do you want to go below the surface?

It is crucial to learn as much about your partner's history as well as you can. This will help you discover their triggers that affect their emotions. It is a fact that our past experiences affect the way we interact with one another. Discuss your experiences from the past to gain a better understanding of the triggers, habits and strengths.

Be compassionate

Your partner's experiencing must be understood by you. Be sensitive even when you do not comprehend them. It is a fundamental an essential part the human condition. Accepting the fears of the other and doubts is not a negative thing. anyone by any means.

Couple Conflict Resolution Techniques

Learning to manage conflict efficiently will guarantee that whenever an argument is triggered, you will be able to resolve it with the proper tools. If you're not adeptly managing conflicts and disagreements minor arguments could get worse and escalate into bigger conflicts. This could cause a huge gap within you as well as your spouse.

Understanding how to manage conflicts and resolution of conflicts within a marriage can be an extremely difficult task since both of you will have to change a lot of negative habits and learn to communicate better. It will take some time and practice therefore, make sure you're open with your spouse and confidence-based. The more considerate you can be of one another the easier it will be to incorporate these new strategies in your disputes and experiencing less arguments, resentment and more forgiveness and resolutions.

Beware of turning disagreements into fights

A great way to deal with disputes within your marriage is to make sure that disagreements don't develop into disputes. The majority of disagreements occur before a fight actually occurs and learning to recognize disagreements aid both of you to prevent them from developing into something much more significant. By incorporating your skills in conflict resolution into the discussion when the conflict begins, you can keep it from escalating. This means that it is less likely to escalate into an actual dispute as well as more likely to get solved.

If you are able to avoid fighting over issues it's simpler to settle disputes. The reason is that the only thing that must be achieved is finding the solution that both you can accept. If the situation turns into a dispute and it escalates, it could cause you to have to recover from the hurt and anger.

Be aware that disagreements do not necessarily mean fighting. A key to avoiding fighting is knowing how to agree without being attacked personally by the conflict. That means, although it is possible to be angry and angry over the dispute however, you should not take it personal. Don't feel that your partner doesn't agree with you, causing hurt to your feelings or cause you to be stressed.

Make sure you fight fairly

If the disagreement escalates into an argument, you need to engage in a fair and respectful manner. Doing something dirty could result in anger, hurt, and anger. If you do end up fighting, try not to point blame, making accusations and judging someone based on their past incidents, or using a portion of someone's life to hurt them. Doing your best to bully your spouse to convince yourself that you're right or hurt them simply because you think they've hurt you is fine. When you do this it is possible to destroy the trust and the intimacy of your relationship and end up unhappy with one another and not able to come up with a solution. This isn't a good situation to be in because it can lead to the absence of a solution or, even more importantly, could cause your marriage to end.

If you've reached an area within your marriage that you are feeling that your arguments are commonplace and that either (or both) of you is inflicting pain on the other It could be beneficial to include a counselor for marriage to the mix. The presence of someone who can moderate your discussions and promote to facilitate communication between your spouse can assist you in beginning the process of healing and learning to talk and debate more well.

Refuse to apologize if you did something Not Right

Do not wait for your partner to make an apology. Instead, if you've committed a mistake acknowledge the error and accept responsibility for what you did. Refusing to apologize when you've committed a mistake suggests that you do not care if you've hurt someone else's feelings or accept responsibility of your behavior. This can lead to your partner feeling that they will never change, and that you'll be in a sour relationship moving forward. In the end, they could lose faith.

If you decide to do something and apologize sincerely for the wrong you've done, it will be more likely that your spouse will be able to forgive you. This is due to you showing that you are aware that you've damaged them and regret it. This shows that you're willing to change your behavior to not hurt them in the same way.

Refuse to apologize if your spouse feels they have damaged their feelings. In the next step, ask them to clarify the way you damaged their feelings and what they can do in order to prevent harming their feelings in the future. This indicates that although you may not be able to comprehend this moment, you're willing to do your best and you are determined to correct the wrongs and be more considerate in the future.

Have a timeout if you Have to

When a disagreement is going on In the event of a heated argument, it's not unreasonable to request an end to the argument. When the situation gets heated and people's feelings are damaged, or you feel like your argument is not working and you are tired, a timeout can be the perfect way to take a break in a calm, grounded state, and be aware of the goals. In general, the aim is to have each party be understood and heard, and for a consensus that can be reached to resolve the conflict with a resolution.

If your dispute has come to the point that there is there is no solution achieved, when you feel that you're not moving forward and your feelings are being damaged, or when you feel like it's growing too much, schedule an end time. Relax and take a moment to let your emotions out and return to a calm and rational space. You can then approach the conversation once your calm has returned.

Explain the real reason you Are Discontent

It is important to explain the main motive behind your reasons for being frustrated or angry. It is essential to be prepared to describe why you're angry and the actions that led to it and how you can resolve it. This helps your friend have the ability to understand the issues being discussed during the discussion.

If you don't make the effort to write down the things you are angry about the person you are with is left to guess. This means that they could conclude that you're upset over something different from what has been causing you pain. In the meantime, they could be arguing regarding a specific topic while you are arguing in a different direction regarding a different subject. This can result in an abundance of confusion.

Be Responsible for Your Feelings and opinions

You are responsible for your thoughts and feelings. Even if you're talking about what you have said, talk about it in a manner that you're discussing your own perspective of the words they used and not about what they were saying. This way, if the things you thought you heard and what they intended to convey were two different things it doesn't appear as if you're feeding the same words.

Be sure you're not taking your feelings and thoughts as the only truth. This means you must are able to recognize that a variety of views, opinions, ideas and beliefs are valid. When you are accountable in by keeping the mind wide open, you can be sure that you're validating your partner.

Be Sure to Break the Barrier of Touch

We often create what psychologists refer to as"a "touch wall" between us and our loved ones. In essence, it's an unconscious barrier is put in place to shield ourselves from hurt that we think the other person will cause us. It can result in us feeling disengaged from our companion but it can also cause a lack of confidence and trust with our partners.

If anyone is hurt due to any reason, it is important to cut off the barrier between you and your companion. It is possible to do this by placing a arm around their shoulders, placing your hands on theirs or even hugging them to show them that you are still there for them even if you do not agree with them right now. Engaging in physical affection during disagreements can remind you and your partner that you're still close and cherish each other. It is also a reminder that your relationship is more than this disagreement and that you are able to overcome it to benefit your relationship's overall good.

Stay focused to the Bigger Picture

If you find yourself fighting between your partner, be aware of the larger view. Sure, you're having an argument however, you're not having an argument. Also your relationship is much greater than the argument you're having. Be aware that although you might be fighting in the present, there is an entire union between you.

Finding a new perspective on your relationship, and understanding that you're both sharing the same purpose can assist your efforts to come up with the best solution. This is because you'll recognize that your disagreement is insignificant compared to what you have in common.

Be respectful of your partner's Viewpoint

Even if you don't agree, you should respect your partner's viewpoint and your partner's. If you don't respect your partner's viewpoint they are deemed unworthy as well as make them feel as if they're not worthy of their own thoughts and opinions. Additionally you make it appear that your approach is the only way to go and that they have to agree with you, or else the solution won't be achieved. This kind of totalitarian attitude can cause anger, hurt and feelings of being ignored and left out by your spouse.

Be sure to show respect for your partner's point of view. Allow them to explain, paying attention to their words and not interrupting even if you do not agree.

Be Real About How You Feel

If you have a dispute between you and your spouse, it is important to remain honest about how you feel. If you are in a heated argument with someone else, it could be very easy to experience difficulty in expressing your feelings. It is possible that you are afraid that your feelings will not be acknowledged or appreciated or that your feelings will make you appear weak. These fears could lead to your avoiding speaking up that ultimately leads to your partner not knowing the exact place you're trying to be.

Make a commitment to finding a solution

When you see an argument or disagreement that has arisen with your partner, you must make the decision to find an answer. If you are determined to find the solution, it becomes more straightforward to argue with respect and be sincere. This is because you're focused on the goals and getting into the trap of fighting in the name of the sake of being right or to cause harm to your friend in the way you believe they're hurting yourself. Instead, you're determined to find ways to communicate in a way that allows you to sense that the conflict has been resolved to your mutual benefit.

If you're not in conflict, tell your partner that this is the primary goal when there is a spark of disagreement. You could also ask them to join in the goals together. So, when there is a disagreement between both of you, you'll know that you're working toward the same goals during the disagreement. This will ensure that you are in a positive frame of mind when you disagree as well as helping you end all disputes and fights in a manner that is sensitive to both of you.

Couple Discord Resolution Exercises

We have been spending a lot of time discussing communication and how crucial it is to your daily life in your marriage, it's time to look at some of the more practical activities you and your partner could make use of to strengthen the lines of communication that exist between you.

Couples-specific communication activities are exercises that couples could utilize to enhance the way they communicate with each other. While working in these activities together communication abilities will improve as each partner will become more aware of each other. When communication improves and improved, not only will the words you use together understood, but also the significance behind them can be comprehended as well.

There are numerous options for communication that you could select to conduct along with your companion. Below, we're going to discuss the most efficient methods that will result in both of you communicating more and connecting better more than you have ever.

Talk about a structured discussion

The first thing we will examine is how to have a an organized discussion with your companion. In order to be successful in this you must take time to chat to your spouse. This should happen where are able to focus on each other, and there is no distractions. Shut off your phones and turn off the computer and ensure that your children are asleep or to the childsitter.

Discuss an issue that the two of you would like to discuss about. Once you have decided on a topic the two of you need to begin to talk. However, instead of talking in the way you usually do you should introduce a little more structure to your conversation. It is possible to add this into your conversation using validation, empathy, and mirroring. It's when you repeat what you partner has said, but using the words of your choice, expressing that you are intrigued and interested.

If you and your partner decide to sit down to have some formal conversations You are ensuring that you are able to be completely alone and focus on one the other. You are paying your attention to the other to observe them, praise their feelings, and sympathize with them. You'll be amazed by how this little gesture will open their eyes to you and help them be more open to what you say to them.

Play games that promote positive language

The next task to be worked on is to play games of positive language. In this case each partner within the relationship should replace any negative language they are using by using more positive words. If you take a moment to take a moment to think about it, you will realize that we all use far too many negative words. It is commonplace to do this in our autopilot mode, without contemplating it. However, the subconscious of the person who is who is in the relationship is likely to be able to detect the information and be aware of negative remarks which are said.

Even if we do not intend to speak in negative terms in our conversations, we're making the other person feel bad. They will feel upset and might begin to feel some discontent towards you. This could cause them to be resistant to any type of interaction with you as they do not want to be negatively all the time. Most of the time the two of you are likely to be doing this to a certain extent. This is why we must concentrate on improving our communication and switch the negative into positive.

When you stop and take time to do this kind of exercise it will make you better aware of many ways you interact with your partner and you might begin to recognize that you're being negative with them. Then, you can change certain negative patterns of communication and begin speaking more positive words.

Have a trip with your loved ones

This may sound like a surprise at first, but organizing and taking an adventure with your spouse can be a wonderful therapy activity to improve your communication. The reason for this trip is the two of you companion are likely to spend at least one day however, it is more often in a fresh and stimulating setting.

A trip with your partner can be a powerful therapy since it allows couples to relax and unwind from the stress and hustle that goes on in their daily life, and provides them with an opportunity to unwind. When you are able to go on a trip, you'll discover that it does amazing things for improving the way you communicate.

Being able to communicate with anyone, not just your partneris likely to be difficult when you're stressed and exhausted. Most of the arguments and miscommunications that you have with your partner happen because one or both are tired and stressed.

If you want to increase the amount of communication within your relationship, be proactive in promoting stress relief to the greatest extent feasible. Once stress is eliminated it lets you and your partner to be focused on one another while talking and connecting on an even deeper level. Planning is beneficial since you and your partner must communicate effectively to ensure that you have the plan in place.

Utilize to apply the Three and Three Method

In this exercise, both parties in the relationship should go to a quiet space and alone, and then make an inventory. This list should comprise three things they love about their partner , and three things they don't like concerning their companion. After you've finished you can get to share your list with each other.

If your spouse begins to go through these lists make sure you thank them for their good quality, the characteristics you listed under the category of likes. Then, discuss the reasons for displeasure and provide the feedback you've got for them with a calm, calm and respectful manner.

You should be cautious about this one. Also, ensure that both of you are in a positive position where they're not angry and will not write down the things they're angry about. They don't have any issues to insult the other person and cause them to feel guilty. They're there to in fostering a dialogue and to ensure that you are able to voice any complaints at an early stage. You should not be able to focus at the other person or bring them down, cause them to feel uneasy or insult them.

The "three and three exercises" is an excellent alternative to try. In many instances, it's going to be among the most effective activities for communication for couples since it outlines what they need to discuss, and the best way to go about it.

Share Your Emotions

Another thing you can focus on while trying to improve the communication between you and your partner is that couples need to talk about their feelings. Couples should take a seat and be in a quiet space so that they don't have interruptions and share the feelings they feel with each the other. If the feelings are buried far in the depths there's going to be plenty of problems that surface.

To foster and support the growth of your bond both of you need to spend time to be supportive of each other, speak about your feelings and talk. If you are finding it difficult to accomplish on by yourself, you might think about going on an event for couples or an intimate retreat. These retreats will be equipped to teach you how to interact with one another. In the end this will help you gain a better understanding of your partner and where they're communicating and will help to strengthen your relationship.

Keep a Journal

This is an excellent option for couples who discover that talking isn't their best characteristic, and may discover writing to be a better method for their needs. Some people express themselves via conversation but others discover that they cannot express themselves in any other manner other than writing.

When you write notes like these take a moment to consider how your loved ones feels when they read these notes. Consider the best way to express yourselfin one that will make them feel happy. Even if you're trying to talk about an issue or provide feedback, figure out how to phrase the entire issue to ensure that your partner doesn't think that you're excluding them or placing them in a defensive position. When you do this, your friend will shut down the communication lines, and it's going to be difficult to open them again.

Play Multi Options

To do this you must have some time treats. You can decide to spend 30 minutes or even an hour with each other and then give your partner several alternatives. You could, for instance, give your partner the option of any of the following:

• A back massage as well as a massage for the shoulders by a long hug.

* Honest and sincere words of praise. genuine praise

* A thoughtful present that is based on the information you know about your loved one and what they enjoy.

* An opportunity to enjoy a more relaxing shower or bath while you tend to your children or wash the dishes later.

* Make sure you spend at least 30 minutes with your partner, and you give your full attention and are free of distractions.

Your partner will then be able to decide which method is compatible with their preferred love language and feels more close to you than they have ever. The more you do this exercise along with your spouse, the greater perception you'll get of your partner's love languages and you'll become more adept at figuring out best ways to keep one your love tanks filled.

Couple Conflict Management

The way that a couple resolves any conflict that may occur will make a huge difference in the happiness that is present in the relationship as well as how long you will remain together. A lot of conflicts will arise within your relationship, particularly when you have been in a relationship for a lengthy period. It is essential that you are able to be a team and get the most effective results from the process.

We all want to live our lives in harmony, constantly being in complete agreement with the people closest to us, and not having any fights or disagreement. Of of course when it comes to having a partner that lives with us, or whom we get to see a lot in the long run there will occasions when we do not agree on things and when things don't turn out as we'd prefer. One of the most effective ways to work through these conflicts is to:

Create an environment that allows for the Open Communication

In any relationship that is healthy the two of you have to be able communicate with each other in a way that is open about what's your biggest issue and what you believe is working. It is not enough to talk about problems when they arise within the relationship. It can become monotonous and cause a loss of the communication between you as you become tired of talking about negative things with each other all the time. It is also important to discuss about the positive aspects in your relationship. This helps the conversation be easier to handle and makes sure that nobody in the relationship is feeling like all they're doing is incorrect. Both parties have the opportunity to speak freely to one the other without judgment and help each other improve their lives.

Make an effort to be respectful Even when Things get Hot

There are instances when your conversations and disagreements can become a little heated. Even when you try to work together and work on issues together, it's not difficult for things to spiral out of control and get hot when you don't intend for them to. However, regardless of this you must keep a manner that is peaceful and respectful throughout the entire process. Do not go over the line at any point and begin making fun of your spouse. You must ensure that your focus is on the present conflict and avoid trying to drag your partner down or make personal jokes.

Be aware of arguments that are more about control

If you think that your spouse is fighting you over wanting to be in control of the way you behave This should be a major signal to them and you may have to seek out assistance. When your spouse is angry about a silly thing like your texting friends who are not your sex counterparts or doesn't like the way you place your school work and other obligations in relation to them, or tries to force you to make a connection with them and limit your time to spend with your friends These are indications you are letting your spouse influence you. Be assertive in these situations and assure them that even though you appreciate them, you have to look after certain other matters.

Do not get involved in an argument over this as your partner might be seeking to control you due to their distrust issues or other issues that could be triggered. If you think this is due to some other issue, it's okay to think through and find out the root of the issue.

Think about whether the issue is something you can resolve or not

Sometimes we have to fight with our partners when it's about some thing that is significant, and will impact our lives. It is important to have large conversations about where you'd like to attend school, whether you would like to have children or not, or the place you would like to reside. They can cause conflict if you discover that you have different objectives and can turn into conflict as you try to find a middle of the road.

Understanding how to resolve the conflict that may are inevitable and being prepared to manage the differences of opinions that are bound to arise could make all the distinction in how the relationship is managed.

Couple Conflict Style

Because of the growing number of arguments people face each day, there is the need to understand how to resolve the issues. It is crucial to know how disputes are created and how they can be resolved. Arguments are a normal part of life However, that does not mean that you can't solve them.

Avoiding

Affronting conflict is a method to end the debate on the subject. Simply put, abstaining from the subject is not discussing it, and is not doing anything to make it more or less so. It's like everyone is living their lives as if the issue has not occurred. There is nothing to be done it's all in harmony.

Affording

Being able to resolve a conflict is beneficial in resolving conflicts. It is when one side is able to comprehend the needs of the opposing side and is willing to compromise. One side will meet the needs of the other side in order to stop the argument. This type of approach is employed in situations where one party believes it is better to be peaceful than win an argument. One side will always concede to the other, while the latter always wins to ensure peace.

Forcing

In order to resolve a conflict, it occurs whenever one of the involved forces decides to exercise formal authority. This could include notifying the boss of the issue, letting him handle the situation or using another authority to resolve the issue. Anything that makes the team in question to give up is considered to be an element of the force strategy.

Collaborating

Working with other teams may help in resolving an issue. This happens the case when two individuals or teams cooperate against one another or an individual. This is similar to asking members who will join you in order to scare the opposing party away. Most often, this happens in schools. When there is a conflict the students pull their peers to join them. In a flash, a simple disagreement turned into a war in the school.

Competing

The competition between two teams or individuals can also solve issues. The majority of the time, there are bets at the heart of a contest, such as the team that loses gives up the argument, and then proves they are correct. This happens most often in the workplace, particularly when there are multiple divisions within that same division. Everyone is working towards achieving the same objective however, the various teams compete against each other.

Compromise

The process of compromise is one way to resolve disputes that may not be a good solution for both parties. Each team member will need the ability to share a portion of the issue. This helps in reducing disagreements. This strategy can help settle any disagreement over competing ideas. The mediator will consider each aspect of the idea that is presented by the teams and combine them to form a completely new concept. In a way, it's like no one is satisfied, but there is no sadness either.

Conflict between Couples

Conflict can be defined as any dispute, which includes disagreements or series of ongoing disagreements over the best way the best to allocate money. Conflict can be very stressful, however it can help to clear out the air' resolve issues that must be resolved. Conflicts and disputes can make us feel angry or even occur because we've become confused regarding some other issue. Perhaps we're trying to manage our anger at work, and to put aside actions that might be regrettable. It is much more likely that we make rude remarks to other people at home due to this unfortunately. It's also less likely that there will be anyone in the vicinity who could mediate, which means that conflicts can get out of hand in a manner that wouldn't happen at work.

The result is that conflict could quickly turn into a very unpleasant and, often, very intimate when a relationship is. We all find ways to hurt others in the presence of others. It could be what we'd like to do when we are angry and regret later.

Talk about your feelings before you are angry and come up with the best way to handle it. It might be beneficial to discuss how you're reacting in times of frustration and assist one another in dealing with that. For instance, if one person is upset It might be helpful to have the other person wait until they can speak later.

Conflicts aren't easy to manage when couples are young, who might be struggling with more recent issues. For couples of a certain age who have been discussing their differences They tend to put aside disputes and focus on more meaningful activities, perhaps because they are taking advantage of their time. The age of the partners appears to be the main reason for this major shift in managing conflict, however this change could be influenced by length of time spent together as couples.

Couples engage in all sorts of exchanges to maintain a level relationship. We'll have to make personal sacrifices to support our relationship while expecting our partners to take similar or similar types of sacrifices. It is a good feeling when the partners agree that there is equilibrium, that is, the amount that we offer is equivalent to the amount we get. However, if one of us thinks that the other gives more than what he or they receive the perceived gap causes a problem for the partner who is shorted and can cause for conflict.

When viewed from this perspective the main reasons behind the happiness of a couple's life could be significant. We are the main vehicle for improving our relationship. If we're unhappy about what our partner does or doesn't do, we must allow ourselves to make our concerns heard by asking them questions. Armed with this information and understanding, couples can take the necessary steps to improve their relationship in order to meet the requirements. Arguments help couples to work as a group to resolve their issues as a couple. And should they be successful by doing this they'll be more committed to each other.

The relationship can be rocky at times where partners feel they cannot be friends. In particular, the process of resolving conflicts or entering a new phase of life, for instance, having a child, can create stress. The stress both partners are juggling during these phases can put stress for the marriage. Some couples might believe that their relationship is suffering from serious issues that are not fixable.

Some may even think they're not happy or in love with one another in the present. It is possible that other people are less argumentative, or have less hate, or are better in tackling their issues as we are. It's perfectly normal to have times of intense conflict. It is a reality for almost every couple and, in this sense, we're likely to be no more or less than the rest of them.

While we don't be aware of what's happening behind closed doors, there's an the possibility that couples we have in our circle are likely to fight just as frequently and as hard like we fight, or even more in the different ways. It's true that those who don't engage in the occasional disagreement could be more prone to issues than those who fight every day. They may struggle with honesty or feel emotionally detached, making their relationships in a superficial way. Sometimes, they avoid conflict due to the belief that their problems aren't solvable or their behavior are such that even minor disagreements could escalate into major disputes.

Some couples, for instance couples who have traditional views on the roles of women and men. are able to avoid certain issues since they are considered to be a matter of the topic, and one of the spouses does not want to alter their beliefs. Whatever the reason the issue is that anything that causes tension can remain unresolved when couples ignore issues in order to avoid conflicts. In the end, unsatisfied partners don't feel they have have the ability to improve their relationship.

Partnerships are lasting relationship. It is possible that you have signed a formal contract to each other. It is essential to collaborate, develop the capabilities, and deal with the differences in your opinion if would like to keep the relationship going. The most important part of this is learning to disagree constructively while also creating an agreement or a partnership. Anyone who has been in a relationship understands that conflicts between partners are inevitable. They can arise due to many reasons, but they are more frequently due to a perceived injustice in the relationship.

It is more clear the reasons why inequality can lead to conflicts through what is known as the social exchange theory. Everyone of us wants to gain such benefits from our partners. We are also aware that if we do get these benefits but there are things equally important that we'll give to our partner in return. In a different way, even though we'd like to give or share with our partner good things, there will be conditions to be fulfilled.

The reasons couples are jealous

It's normal to feel at times when you are in a romantic relationship. It's true that every one of us at one point in our relationship has felt the awkward feeling of jealousy. At times we are jealous because of the feeling that there's a threat to the relationship with a different person, as well as the fear that a loved person could find a new one to take over our place. While most people only experience occasionally and with a little jealousy, some experience it to a sever extent. The most common reaction to jealousy is to break up the relationships when you are in a highly jealous pattern.

Insecurity

One of the primary motives for jealousy is fear. There are many times when people talk about the term "inferiority complex" that is not an actual psychological term, but rather refers to an poor self-esteem or a deficient ego. someone who is jealous and feels unsecure within his intimate relationships such as: isn't sure if he's attractive enough and attractive enough to keep someone engaged with him for a long the course of time. It's important to keep in mind that vulnerability for both women and men isn't always complete. That is an individual may be brilliant and extremely efficient at work, yet their psychological disorder (becoming jealous) results from their relationships with intimate partners. People can be deeply unsecure when it comes to their relationships with loved ones.

Insufficient Trust

It is possible for jealousy to cause problems for romantic relationships. Trust is a crucial element of any stable and good relationship. The act of jealousy can trigger doubt, distrust and anger that can escalate into extremely extreme emotions and behaviours. There is a risk of becoming anxious about the possibility of being betrayed. We may begin actively checking out our partner or friend and try to uncover their deceit. We could become a bit obsessed. What began as a non-equity partnership could turn into a tense bond between a guard and a jailer. Perhaps, feeling a hint of jealousy can be an indication that something you should pay attention to is happening in your relationship. A certain aspect of the relationship isn't going as you'd like it to. This means that our emotions are able to overpower reasoning and logic.

Conflict also offers the opportunity to learn more about your partner and enjoy them more. Be able to look at disagreements as an opportunity to change something more than just a reason to retreat. If you find yourself in a situation where you are at odds with your partner and are unsure what you can do to salvage your relationship, look for the positive instead of being unhappy and feeling jealous, and commit to working with your partner to create a safer future.

Conflict between Siblings

Irregular rivalries between siblings are common when you have more than one child. The issue of rivalries gets more difficult when any of the children begins inflicting pain on the other. The nature of the problem is increased when one child tries to take over another child.

Rivalries between siblings are difficult to deal with and it can be very difficult for siblings to endure all of this. Accept the fact that fights and jealousies are commonplace in families. Learn to teach your children how to deal with the emotions that accompany the petty fights and arguments.

Unfairness, feelings of victimhood shouldn't go along with sibling rivalries within the family. It is important to distinguish an unhealthy sibling rivalry as distinct from the normal rivalry. The structure of a bullying victim setting is:

The children (usually the one who is older) is bullied by the other kid.

With their power and strength the bully will always try to target his younger brother.

To retaliate against these attacks, the one who has been the subject of bullying will resort to violent methods to stop the bully.

The victim usually takes back their revenge when they call the bully kid by calling him names.

* If the issue becomes physical, it means that both suffer from serious issues with their thought processes and are self-doubting.

* You have to be able to hold both the bully as well as the victim accountable whenever an argument or conflict breaks out. Ask questions like "Why do you believe that it's acceptable to hit your

sister or brother?" and "Don't you think that rules are relevant even when you're angered?" You can fight and challenge their faulty thinking method by asking these kinds of questions.

Every sibling fight are as a two-way battle, and both kids to be accountable for their actions. If you can determine that the fight began due to both of them, you must always take both of them responsible.

Establish strict rules and penalize both parties should they get involved in unnecessarily. Inform them that you do not care who initiated the fight and what caused it. Separate the two of them and ask them to be on their own for a couple of minutes, and then talk to them individually.

By utilizing Bickering Tables Concept of a Bickering Table

Arguments over bickering, such as insufferable fights and constant back and forth disputes are the main causes of competition within your home. You should think about creating a bickering area.

* Plan a bit of your time to both kids.

* Tell them to sit at the table, and discuss against each other for a long time.

* They have to discuss and debate without justification every day.

* They'll stop doing it over and over again since they will recognize that it's foolish to fight and argue in the name of nothing.

* Even when they don't have much to debate ensure that they are in the room until scheduled time has passed. You must stop yourself from calling the fight to a referee:

It is not advisable to get in the middle of a sloppy dispute or fight when it's not serious. Do not be a referee if you are not required to. If you find yourself into the middle and you are weighed down with the obligation of deciding the right side and who's wrong.

Instead of judging and refereeing rather than letting the children understand that there must be no fighting within the house. There are severe consequences should you spot a problem with a sloppy motive.

Make sure you schedule each child's schedule to have their time to relax and unwind. Be sure that breaks don't overlap with one another. If your children are a bit volatile toward one another when they play it is best to set distinct times when they can play.

In a bid to end jealousy

Parents often pay more attention to children who is the victim of the fights and disputes between siblings. This is a problem because you're rewarding your child for being an innocent victim.

Always strive to be kind and praise both of each of them equally. They feel a sense of love when they receive praise from your. Give small praises to each other. If you are able to give compliments to one another equally the likelihood of jealousy creeping into the relationship is significantly smaller.

Empathy to the situation

The primary goal of disciplining your children is giving them the necessary tools to live success in life. One of the most important tools you can give to them is empathy. Learn with your kids how important it is to be empathetic to others. Let them know how unkind and rude behavior could impact someone else in the world. Let them think about the things they're trying to accomplish. Be sure to teach them the importance of having empathy for everyone, even relatives.

Understanding Which War to Take on and which ones to avoid

Find out which one is a danger to enter and which one you should be quiet about. Let them deal with small squabbles and disputes on their own. Make sure you inform them of the consequences should the situation gets out of control. Inform them that you will expect to figure the problem out on their own. Be clear about the consequences if they continue going back to the same issue repeatedly. Do not ignore minor issues, but address more serious problems. Be sure to speak up when you witness any type of physical or verbal abuse in a fight or argument.

Reminding yourself that You Do Not Have to Treat All of Them equally

It is impossible to treat children in a fair way. It is important to take the child's age the child is born in, their birth order and the conflict before finding the best solution. Be aware that your children aren't identical, so it is impossible to expect flawlessly synced and behaviour from each of them. Take your gutsy decision at every turn.

Reducing Comparisons between the Kids

It is not a good idea to make that your child is inferior when you compare one to one. This is a negative parenting sign and you should not use it. If one of your children does something well, ensure that you congratulate them. Do not compare the result with your other child in order to create an inferiority.

Children are already compared with many in the school environment and in society. Every action and every performance are evaluated in relation to the threshold that is considered to be the most effective. They are already being put under pressure and you shouldn't do the similar.

The ability to listen to Both Sides of the Story

Children argue and get along one another from time to the time. Make sure to shield the growing body of your child from physical assaults from each other. It is also important to ensure that your children don't suffer emotional harm.

If a fight turns physical, you must ensure that you are able to break up the siblings first. After that, you need to bring the fight under control and get it under control. If you observe that your child is engaging in verbal abuse You should stop it.

You must ensure that your children do not have emotional scars to their lives, since it takes a great deal of time to recover. Be open to the two aspects of the story, and take them to task equally if you are able to. Allow your children to let out their frustration in the appropriate location at the right time before they can resolve the issue. In those moments they'll be overwhelmed by their own feelings in their heads. They won't pay attention to what you're talking about. Make sure that they're attentive to your instructions on the ground rules following the fight.

Conflict between parents and children

If a parent is faced with the stress of a situation, and their child is in need of attention, the stress could trigger a rapid response. Parents may not think about the solutions or actions, even if they are able to think as their minds are racing. Parents sometimes forget how to treat their feelings despite trying to shield them.

If your child is shouted at or beaten by any means, they'll require your assistance. You could accidentally help a child learn to tolerate violence. If you are able to acknowledge your child's feelings and react to verbal abuse, confirm the child's experiences. You will teach them the appropriate response and encourage your child to honor their emotions.

If you observe children who are engaging into verbal abuse, consider one of these suggestions. These are suitable for various situations and for different age groups. Find out how they can meet your requirements:

* "That kind of discussion is not acceptable."

* "I do not want to hear this kind of conversation."

* "That kind of conversation does not inspire me to be awestruck by you."

* "That's enough."

* "There'll never be such conversations at my house."

If a child is victimized or witnesses abuse, that child suffers. As children age under the pressure of abusive situations they can display their anger, sadness and confusion, or even eliminate the experience with alcohol or other destructive means. If children do not grow up in a loving and peaceful home, having both parents at family does not mean that it is more healthy.

If you divorce with your partner, the child has to be able to communicate their feelings regarding this to you. Children can say "I dislike the person you are," meaning that he or she is angry about what happened. The expression "I dislike you" isn't verbal abuse. It's a powerful expression of emotion. It is possible to hear this while you're feeling most vulnerable. However, if your child is upset due to the changes that have occurred in your relationships, it is important to acknowledge the feelings of your child.

Whatever similarities there may be in genetic makeup there is no way to say that two children are identical. There might be some commonalities in the emotional and physical needs of children within similar age however, they all have distinct personality traits. Their personalities dictate their preferences and dislikes, their manner in which they integrate, and the way they react.

Common Parenting Conflicts

* Temper tantrums This is a nerve-wracking experience to see your child

develop the habit of throwing temper out in public areas. It is crucial to determine the root of the problem, such as being exhausted, hungry, or over-stimulated or has a desire for to do something. A child who is having a temper tantrum can start crying and cause chaos, not let him calm down or pay attention to the child, and avoid expressing the cause.

* Disobedience is one of the problems parents have to deal with when they have children. It could become a habit that lasts for a lifetime If not stopped in the bud.

* Aggression A child who is violent with others exhibits violent reactions or damages objects, which can be very distressing. If not dealt with promptly, this could be an unhealthy habit that could result in more serious issues with your child the other parents in the vicinity.

Bad eating practices: Due to the ease of access to junk food and a variety of food choices Many children are suffering from poor eating habits, which deprive of the essential nutrients they require.

* Addiction to Modern Technology A frequent use of devices and internet technology creates the constant challenge of parents and their children.

• Lack of enthusiasm to study or to complete homework When your kid suddenly displays lack of interest in his studies or puts off completing homework, then he's likely to be struggling in his studies or paying focus is diverted to other activities such as video games.

* Lying: The majority of children are caught lying which is a type of lie that causes real harm. The majority of the time, they are unaware they're lying. They're trying to hide from the situation. But, if you let lying to persist, it could lead to more serious and more serious lies, such as keeping important details or facts from yourself. If lying becomes a habit and routine, it could become a part of the child's character.

* Whining If your child is in the habit of complaining or complaining about minor things the child is trying to get your attention.

* Insecurity: If your child avoids social interaction, is aloof or doesn't want to be around other kids they could be struggling with confidence issues.

Don't be scared to make mistakes and fail. Do not blame yourself too heavily for not meeting the expectations of others and develop your own parenting strategies to help your children. If you observe him copying your bad habit be sure to alert him and work with him to fix the issue.

Each child has a distinct variety of issues when he transitions from infanthood to adulthood. The task of getting him to eat a healthy foods, disciplining him the right way to match the personality of your child, informing the child on sexuality as well as teaching him the right values, and so on will be an integral element of your life when you embark on your journey of parenting. Keep in mind that there aren't any hard as well as fast techniques to parent children. There aren't any absolute solutions either. All you require is a warm heart with an open mind and a constant effort to be the kind of parent your child will see as an example of positive behavior.

The best way to parent is to accept the fact that your children and you are distinct individuals, each with different personalities. As he ages and you can't solve all his issues to help him transition into adulthood. It's all about learning from your mistakes - both your child as well as your own. If you don't manage the situation properly the first attempt, stop getting yourself in a bad mood and attempt it again. If you commit a mistake in the emotional moment or you feel overwhelmed, take yourself from the situation and get a time-out. After you have cooled down then go back and apologize thank you to your kid and after which you can work together to work through the issue. Your attitude towards yourself will give your child a sense of how to overcome mistakes.

Chapter 10: Couple Relationships

Communication And Conflict

Resolution

It is essential to ensure that your relationship is healthy. Without it the passion and love in your relationship will turn stagnant and cold. Communication is like oxygen for relationships. Many people believe that it's all about simply listening attentively however there is additional to this.

Communication Doesn't Have to Be Just Verbal

Communication isn't only spoken, but also. The facial expressions used in various situations are likely to be the exact same. There are a variety of non-verbal signals. Understanding the way that both genders utilize these signals will alter the way both of you interact with one another in a positive way. In this way, you will better understand your spouse's hopes, goals desires, fears, and needs without any miscommunication. Let's take a look at these non-verbal signals mean.

Physical contact

No matter what the nature of their genetic makeup gender, males and females have a different way of communicating through touch. While for males, heavy physical slaps and rude nudges can be a method of showing camaraderie, influence, power and power females take the more gentle approach of giving an embrace and reaching to stroke the other's shoulder to show empathy or avoiding touching when they are you are not feeling well or upset or wronged the way.

Through research and lots of study, we now understand that touch triggers releases of the hormone oxytocin that causes couples to connect to feel more confident in their relationship and each other regardless of how awful their lives have been. Sometimes, it's not Advil you require however, but a big hug.

* Expressions of the face Human faces are an amazing thing. There are 43 distinct facial muscles capable of producing a multitude of expressions, the closest and most recent estimate being around 10,000. Human facial expression is an extremely significant non-verbal ways that we communicate.

A lot of women make use of numerous facial expressions. Eye contact, or absence of it. There's nodding of the head and lips pursing a much more than males. Along with being able to make a variety different facial expressions females are usually better at interpreting facial expressions because of their expressive and sensitive nature. If you're not convinced then try lying to an individual female. In the majority of cases it won't be time before you're discovered.

"Paralinguistic" communication. Have ever wondered how the word or phrase could mean a variety of things based on the way it's spoken? If yes, you probably have been involved in the concept of paralinguistic communication.

Also known as "paralanguage," it is the study of tone, voice as well as the various subtleties and signals that accompany words when they are spoken. They can be used to represent aspects of communication that transcend words.

A body's posture As men generally tend to have more space in their personal lives than females They tend to position their bodies in where their feet appear spread apart, with their arms further from their bodies, which can make them feel uncomfortable or feel apprehensive. However females are more likely to retract and keep their arms in a tight position with the feet crossed when they are feeling intimidated or fearful towards a particular person or circumstance.

You must be cautious when reading body language. Pay attention to the context that you are observing it. Don't believe that your wife is angry at you for hugging her self--it may be just the cold weather for her.

Reasons for miscommunication in the Relationship

He versus she is a complex

Although women communicate to establish connections and build intimacy, males aren't sure what the rationale behind it. Men consider that communicating should be based on a clear purpose, and see no value in communicating in the absence of being able to resolve any issue.

If a woman informs her husband how she's overweight and is finding it difficult to shed the weight post-baby, a typical response from a male would be similar to, "I have the number of a top personal trainer" or "Why do you not cut back on the fries?" These remarks could be an attack on her appearance however, he really believes the need to offer some advice. The only thing a woman would like is to hear that she is beautiful, no matter the number on the scale.

Passive or active listening? It's an Herculean task to convince most men to be able to listen without having to contribute an idea or a feeling on the issue. Another problem is what to say in every situation. What is the right amount of excessive? Before an individual responds to the question or recounts an event, he's gone through the events that occurred in his head. At the final, he gets to tell the parts which he feels are related to his story.

It's the opposite for the other gender. Women utilize the power of words to express their feelings and feelings fully. There are occasions that a woman might not know what she's feeling or the reason for it until after she's spoken about it. The worst option is to not react when a woman discusses her thoughts and feelings with you. It's easy to think that you're listening to her, which is sufficient, but this isn't the situation. Make sure you know her by putting yourself into her shoes and feeling how she's feeling.

The differences in communication explain the reason why a person becomes reclusive and retreats to the place that he is comfortable. This man cave functions as an escape from the additional costs associated with tickets. In the comfort of his own private space, he focuses on his feelings and attempts to figure out what he's experiencing.

The withdrawal phase may leave his partner thinking that she's responsible or if she is losing the relationship. It's not always the scenario. If confronted with a stressful or challenging circumstance, women will appreciate the amount of support and affection and care from her partner. She will use words to express and understand her emotions.

Avoiding Misunderstandings

After the complexity of communication is understood and I've clarified that gender differences increase the complexity of communication I'd like to emphasize that this doesn't mean that men and women cannot get together. It is possible to get along. It's just a matter of practicing and the desire to be able to communicate with each other.

The main goal of improving communication within your marriage or in your relationship is to learn from the style of communication of each other instead of completely altering the person who is in conflict. Here are some things you should keep in mind if need to be able to communicate effectively with your partner:

* Be aware that communication can be described as having distinct and distinctive styles and each has its own strengths and flaws. Learn these differences and don't be impulsive to point out flaws or finger at someone else.

* Do your best to not fit in or reinforce the stereotypes associated with gender-based differences. Be aware that the environment is a major factor in how you respond either verbally or non-verbally.

* Be aware of and obtain details on the various ways of communicating to manage your responses to each efficiently. Be aware of the various styles and adjust easily to the different styles.

Conflict Avoidant Couple Affair

Betraying someone is one of the most frightening nightmares that anyone can experience. The consequences could be catastrophic. The entire beliefs are shaken upon first glance. A variety of emotions are triggered and involuntary thoughts begin to occupy your thoughts. The question is a constant theme for those who have been betrayed "but what is the reason." It is often followed by suspicions. Even if someone happens to be aware and ready to confront the devil the impact is always severe. It's like a storm when you realize the time who you entrusted in the knowledge that they've cheated you.

You're experiencing a variety of intense emotions, and you are constantly thinking and feel deeply wounded in your heart. Do not feel overtaken by the post-traumatic stress. The person loses sleep, is unable to focus, loses weight and is taken to extremes and suffer from depression or thoughts of ending their lives. In a perfect world, no person would want to have to deal the emotional pain that can occur when someone cheats on you. However, it's the reality. Conversations that are honest and open should precede looking for an extramarital relationship.

When we select someone to be with and then bind ourselves with them, they might decide to remain in relationships that are unhealthy even when there is a problem. If there is an act of deceit by the other party, the one who has been cheated upon is suffering from emotional distress at a fundamental level. When the victim becomes conscious of the deceit it is a traumatic experience. The initial reaction could go as far as running off from shock or closing yourself down, refusing to accept the unfaithful person who is dismissing the issue and claiming it is a miscommunication or a blatant overreaction on your part.

If you are a person who is unfaithful is exposed, it could result in them having to deal with a fight or freeze, or even a flight away from their spouse. Both the unfaithful as well as those who have been betrayed suffer the pain, confusion and a flurry of emotions that have to be handled. The more committed couples are and the stronger the intensity of their grief. It's thrilling to realize that, after being abandoned the couple is open to all the world. Refusal and anger, bargaining, moments of acceptance, are revolving within the mind of the betrayed. Bargaining is a term used to describe the revolving thoughts of "what-ifs.' Unfaithful people may experience the feelings of loss well. If they see their partner's behavior and causing trouble, they might believe that the relationship is over and irretrievable.

If the person who is unfaithful witnesses their spouse is swayed by the situation, after discovering that they are lying, they might discover that the person who was person who was cheated has turned into a cautious. They start to doubt everything and seek safety. They might become resentful to feelings of abandonment. They may become hypersensitive to any future conversation between their cheating spouse.

Make Up for Your Faults

If they are confronted with more information they may be overwhelmed and cause them to react or not respond at all in the interval of 10 to 20 minutes. The reaction to each tiny detail can be extremely or a bit of massive information may trigger no response from the person suffering. They must be strong to make the person who has been harmed feel secure in those times of panic and primal fear.

Your next consideration should be how you can assist them. Try not to be defensive. Accept your mistakes. It is a difficult thing to do because someone else could be engaging in fights, and the normal reaction to fights is to defend. Do your best to be kind to the person. There must be a discussion process between the hurting partner and the unfaithful partner to learn their feelings more. The idea of trying to increase the comfort of their partner is a must. Simply be there alongside them and support them with their discomfort.

Another reaction is to flee after being confronted by the circumstances. This could mean an emotional or physical disappearance that is when the individual is completely silent before you. In the moment, they might be a fear of hurting or doing something to betray the cheating spouse. This desire to give the money back to the cheating spouse is almost unavoidable. Unfaithful spouses may believe that their relationship is coming to an end.

They might interpret it as the most important signal that their partner is going to run away and will easily leave, but it could be just an approach to deal with the trauma of the pain. It's a safety-seeking response. They're only confronting the adversity caused by the circumstance. The pendulum of emotion where they desire to be intimate the day before and the next day, they wish to end their relationship and bring their children away from their betraying spouse. These are all reactions triggered by the adrenaline rush that occurs in various phases of time.

Switch Your Focus

The focus should shift to what the person who has been cheated on can do after a shady partner can cause your feelings to get in the way of your thinking. It's normal to feel confused. Get yourself out of the feeling of numbness and feel these sensations. Do not try to suppress any feelings you experience. A heightened emotional state is not beneficial or help you in any manner. Write or record the emotions you're experiencing. You can take a break. You can go to your own space. If you live together it is the best to get out of the house for a while.

If you're in a relationship that is long-term do not talk to someone who isn't faithful. You might want to stay clear of social media. Avoid following them, or putting your photos together, and make sure to keep your thoughts off of it. Do not do anything outrageous. A makeover or joining the gym to stay in shape is not unusual. Be careful not to criticize your spouse, cause an uproar within the family, or seek divorce in the first instance. The urge to do this could lead you to regret it later. It is not to be taken as an indication of forgiveness or acceptance. This should be carefully contemplated to ensure that the safety of the one who was victim more than the cheating partner. There isn't way to get revenge in absolute terms. It could be temporary and make you feel better but it can do damage that is more harmful than beneficial. The ultimate revenge is to soak the entire situation and making the person who did the wrong apologize for themselves.

Get for help

Get help from a professional to manage the discomfort. It's difficult to recover from the pain and stress that is caused by the loss of your beloved one's actions within a day. It is possible to rely on a trusted friend or parents, or if do not feel comfortable discussing the details of your personal life shared, see an therapist. Let your feelings be heard and begin the healing process. Think about getting better. Stay clear of negative thoughts, and most importantly, stay away from things that remind you of them. It's not easy to accomplish but it's necessary. Let it out, be active on it, take pleasure in socializing with group of friends, go out for late hours, dance hard and plan a trip and purchase something you've always wanted to, but had been putting off. The goal is to restore your spirit and soul without causing any harm to your well-being. Do not contact the family members of their loved ones or their closest acquaintances. You should allow enough time until you can see the person you met previously.

It might even require you getting back on your feet. Don't look for someone else immediately. However, once you've got past this, you can get moving forward in your life. You could connect with someone experiencing the same heartbreak. Try to find an opportunity to overcome and improve the circumstance.

If it's difficult to accept the situation, instead of taking a step towards something catastrophic take the time to figure out why the relationship failed. If you're in a relationship that ended in failure with someone who's believed to be cheating and then the blame is on you. The primary focus is to go back and search for the signs and motives that you believe caused the deceit. It's rarely a one-way flow. In a relationship, both parties have not been able to meet the requirements of the other. It is possible that your relationship will be saved, even if it appears to be in the distance right now. In the chaos, do not overlook the actions of your spouse currently.

The difficult part of having to face the person you love and engaging in dialogue with them is a nightmare. You must have talks with your partner in order to determine if they are planning to save their marriage. Sometimes, the person who was betrayed is in anger because of a need to discuss the lengths that the partner who was not faithful was able to go to, and refuse to reveal the details or not want to apologize. If you're wondering why they haven't provided you with the information you would like to know, do not take it the hard way , and don't dwell on self-doubt. If someone is unfaithful, omitting the details is the worst act they could do in the present. It's enough for them to have broken their spouse's heart and still refuse to give them the information they're entitled to.

The partner who has been cheating is likely to be embarrassed or the circumstances are too difficult to talk about and they may believe that you aren't in a position to deal with the situation. If the person who was betrayed attempts to piece the pieces together it is not an attempt to make you look bad. They're just trying to put of the elements together. A person who is unfaithful doesn't like talking about their affair or addiction, his choices and suffering because it's uncomfortable. But, the spouse who has been cheated is unable to heal unless he or she is able to discuss what has occurred.

Another reason they should keep their distance is because there might there is more than what they have previously acknowledged to. They fear they'll have a lower chance of any restoration in the event that they reveal all the pieces missing. To avoid this, the person who has been swindled must make sure that they take in all information before jumping into any conclusions. It can be painful to contemplate however, if you wish to be fully transparent it is something you have to agree to.

How can you settle a Couple Conflict?

Conflict in relationships are solvable however, they need to be willing to participate in the process. If one or both of the couples do not agree to resolve the dispute, the relationship could be dissolved. There are steps that couples should be able to take to end conflict in their relationship.

Be Prepared to Talk about

First, it is to have couples be willing to talk about the relevant issues and try to settle these issues. If couples aren't willing to engage in a dialogue to resolve the issue will not be possible.

Dialogue is the only way to resolve any disagreement. If you and your spouse are willing to discuss the issues that affect your relationship, the higher the chance of solving the issues. I will just say that regardless of the arrangement for discussion is reached, all parties must be on the same page to ensure the discussion produce results. Each must follow the rules below as the discussion continues.

Every partner must turn to speak and voice their frustrations. The two partners should not speak simultaneously. In the event of conflict, understanding won't be achievedand a second dispute could ensue.

Every partner should listen with intense attention when one is speaking. The phones should be turned off, and any distractions should be kept to a minimum. Any attempt to interrupt when someone is speaking should be done only with permission.

Avoid arguments and using offensive words during your reconciliation talk. You can freely express your opinions without ever insulting the other person or making them feel uncomfortable. The choice of words and the way you express them should be considered and respectfully addressed with respect and respect.

Be objective

When you speak about your relationship with your significant other, it is important to remain neutral. In other words, you must try to look at the issues being discussed from the point of viewpoint, not just your personal opinion. In the absence of this, it will make the discussion pointless. Always remember that you are a human being and you will not always be the right person in every situation. Do your best to determine what you are hearing from your spouse, and you're in the wrong. Look over the words as your partner talks to get to the bottom of the issue.

Admit Your Fault

The man transferred the blame onto his wife. The wife delegates the responsibility of her error on to the snake. Who is the serpent to be blamed? The blame game from the beginning didn't solve the issue of the initial marriage. Instead, it scatters it. They were removed in Eden. Garden of Eden. In any dispute that is fought, both parties will be accountable in one way or another. To end the conflict each party must acknowledge their error before God and one another. Only then, the reconciliation actions be successful.

If you really cherish your relationship and feel you are the one to decide destiny in your relationship, set your ego aside and admit that you weren't all that right. Nothing is lost by doing this. It's a display of maturity and honesty to acknowledge your mistakes and start the process of healing within your relationship.

Apologize

One of the most powerful words that can help heal and solve conflicts within the relationship between you is saying "I apologize" quick and powerful, however often people are unable to do so because of pride won't admit the words to their partner. If you have admitted to the fault of your partner it is normal to say sorry. If you are required to sit down to apologize, do so to prevent your relationship from falling apart.

Forgiveness

It is essential to accept forgiveness from your partner and be able to move on. If you aren't willing to let your partner go, you're not at the right place to make peace. The act of forgiveness not only solves the issue, but also helps you emotionally, physically as well as psychologically. It gives a new perspective to your life as well as your partner. It's difficult to forgive, but it is achievable with the help of God forgiving. It is essential to have mutual forgiveness to allow conflict to be settled. Let the offence go from your heart. It is better for you if you let it go.

Ground Shift

Parties should be willing to alter their views on topics that are being discussed. In a situation where you remain in your position, it is not helpful to the reconciliation process. A win-win-win-win-

win-win-win-win-win- implemented. A slight bend here and there among the parties is what can repair the damaged bridges that exist in the relationship. Do not insist that it be entirely your way. Be flexible and considerate in your choices to ensure both you and your spouse can work out a solution and re-connect.

Renew Your Engagement to Your Partner

After having apologized, being forgiving and rearranging your reasons, the final step is to renew your promise to you and your spouse. Rights and privileges that you denied your partner of the privilege of releasing it. Reiterate your love for your spouse anew and then back it up by doing something.

A warm hug, kiss and holding each other's hands will restore the emotional bond you shared prior to. Simply laugh about every little thing and you'll be back to normal.

Fear of abandonment in Couple Conflict

The fear of being abandoned is thought to be a result of childhood deprivation or trauma. The fear of abandonment has been studied in a variety of ways. The theories behind the fear of losing are interruptions to the natural development of children's emotional and social capabilities in relation to their past interactions and personal experiences and the sensitivity to expectations and notions.

Although it's not a recognized phobia the fear of abandonment an extremely common and destructive fears. People who are afraid of abandonment persist in exhibiting compulsive behavior and patterns of thinking that affect their relationships which could lead to the rejection they worry about becoming a reality.

Our actions and attitudes in our relationships today are thought to be the result of past experiences and lessons that were learned during adolescence. There are a variety of theories for the reason behind our fear of being abandoned. It is possible that you are concerned about being uncomfortable within an intimate relationship. There are times when you struggle in confidence and you think too many thoughts about your relationship, that you become wary of your companion.

A few people are afraid of losing a significant other. There are many fears that they could suddenly find themselves alone. To understand how those who fear losing their loved ones can manage relationships, here's an outline of the ways in which a normal relationship could start and grow.

Getting-to-Know-One-Another Phase

At this point there is a feeling of security. You're not yet terribly interested in the other man but you're living your life and enjoying time with your beloved companion.

Honeymoon Period

That's where you'll want to sign a pledge. You start investing a lot of energy in another person. you really live your life to the fullest and then you start to feel fantastic.

True Wedding

The unique first night period of time can't last for a long time. No matter how well two people get along in real life, the process isn't finished away. Some people fall ill, suffer from issues with their families, start working longer hours, contemplate funds and take time to finish their work.

Although this is a normal and positive stage in relationships, it could be difficult for someone who has the fear of losing their job and may view this to be an indication that the person in question has decided to leave.

The Slight

Men are unique. They are flawed and have faults, dispositions and things that go on their minds. Whatever the extent to which they are concerned about another it is not their responsibility and should not be expected to keep them in the forefront of their minds.

In particular, after the evening timeframe is over it is likely that there will be a slight appearance. It could also be an unanswered instant message an unanswered phone call, or even a supplication for a few days on its own.

Response

If you are one of those who risk unlucky events, this can be the moment that will define you. When you feel nervous you might be convinced that this could be a sign that your spouse has changed their mind about you. The next step is controlled by the fear of misfortune, its force and the individual's to adapt their strategy.

Many people struggle with this issue by being stubborn and controlling, insisting that their loved ones show affection by performing the same actions. Some walk away, refusing their loved ones and being recognized. However, there are those who acknowledge that the fault is theirs and strive to become the role of a "decent sweetheart" with the intention to prevent the other person from going away.

It's not an unimportant one, but it is certainly not a minor one. Sometimes, people do things that people who aren't able to like. In a healthy relationship, one needs to be aware of the reason it's a common reaction that is hardly or anything to have to do with the relationship. In the other hand there could be a feeling of anger over it, but take it in stride with the silence of a conversation or quick declaration. In any event it's unlikely that a single incident will transform into a dominant power on the emotions of the other person.

The Partner's Perspective

Your partner's sudden shift in your attitude seems to be going in the wrong direction. If your spouse does not experience the negative effects of fear of leaving and isn't any clue as to the reason his already amiable partner is suddenly suddenly becoming concerned and challenging, or becoming close or clingy.

Similar to phobias, it's tough to justify or speak up for others due to the fear of being abandoned. Whatever number of times your partner attempts to persuade you, it's not enough. In the end your personality traits and moody reactions may cause a rift with your spouse, resulting in the exact suspicion you most fear.

Adapting Techniques

If your stress is mild and generally controlled If you're in a good place, you be able to gain some peace by considering the situations and contemplating alternative social methods. For many people, however the fear of being abandoned is a root cause of deep-seated issues which are difficult to solve on their own.

Expert help is also needed in order to get over this anxiety in order to gain the self-confidence to transform your feelings into behaviours. While addressing the fear is crucial, it is important to also create the feeling of belonging. Instead of focusing all your energy and time on one individual be focused on creating an environment that is a community.

No one can handle all our concerns or satisfy all our demands. In any event an extensive circle of close friends can play a major role for us in the course of our life.

A lot of people are afraid of distance due to the fact that they do not feel as if they were part of the feeling of having a "clan" or "family" as they were growing in. They are "extraordinary" or disengaged from the people around them due to reasons they don't know. But the good aspect is that it's not always over the point of the point of no return.

In our current world this is a list of your interests, inclinations and goals. Take note of others who have similar characteristics.

Although it is evident that it isn't the case that every person who expresses enthusiasm will turn into an old friend, sharing desires, goals and interests are an excellent way to build an encouraging and strong bunch of friends. Accepting your preferences gives you the confidence that you're able to handle whatever life throws in at you.

If you are aware of the fear of loss, there are certain things you should make to continue recovering. Discuss with the other side about your fears of loss and the way it got there. Let them know where you're at But don't let them resolve your fears of abandonment. Don't ask for more than what is reasonable.

Try to keep your partnerships in place and build your social network. A close relationship will increase your self-esteem as well as your sense of belonging. If you find it difficult to manage try talking to one of our expert advisers. It is possible to benefit from one-on-one contact.

Codependency

Codependency is a harmful relationship that involves an individual who has voluntarily allowed an individual, usually one who is addicted, or who has emotional manipulative disorder be in control and have influence over them. In a codependent relationship, there is an unfair sharing of love, respect trust, care, and love that is given and received. The people who are dependent have self-centered, self-absorbed or addicting friends and romantic partners who cause them to feel unloved and dissatisfied. Even though they hate the people they love and their feelings however, they're unable to alter their lives. Since leaving may not be an option, those who are codependent put everything on the line to win the respect, approval, and affection of their loved ones and fail to achieve some control over their behavior. A person may feel that they're not good enough or worthy of their partner is in need of them. The codependent person feels satisfaction from feeling valued, and their partner is satisfied because they have everything they need. The needs of the person who is codependent are satisfied by their partner regardless of whether they attempt to make their partner fulfill them.

The Signs of Codependency

It can be difficult to tell if someone is codependent from one who is simply emotionally attached. To resolve a codependency issue, they must understand what the codependent behavior is. The signs and symptoms of codependency can vary based on the way in which the individual became dependent.

* Don't Say "No"

* Self-esteem Issues

* Weak Boundaries

* You must have control

* Do not confuse love with pity.

"Being Deluded"

The desire to be loved induces a codependent to entering or remaining in a relationship that requires to be cared for. If they are able to provide their partner with everything they've wanted, the person who is codependent is often praised by the person who is taking them. This plays a significant role in how takers manage to keep their partners around, and the way they ensure they will always be there for them. If the codependent is doing all the things that the person they are taking to do, the taker cannot learn to take care of those tasks independently. The taker's sense that they are entitled is increased as self-esteem and the need to be validated are harmed more. Many years of mental, emotional and even physical violence, as well as manipulative behavior, have huge impacts on both the dependent and their users.

The detrimental effects of being dependent are usually evident later in the course of. Sure, a person who is codependent is obsessed with their obligation to look after their partner however, how does this cause lasting damage to one's life? This fixation is a sign of codependency. The effects are the outcomes that these relationships and symptoms cause that could alter the future of the codependent. To better understand the distinction between symptoms and effects, think of codependency as an alcoholism drinking every day as a symptom. alcohol-related liver disease as a result of being an alcohol dependent.

What Causes Codependency?

It is a learned habit and is passed on through generations. It is crucial to know what kind of situations could lead to a person developing codependency so that you can stop this vicious cycle from affecting many more people. In addition to dysfunctional families, unhealthy relationships can cause the person to become dependent or even the companion of an addict that was initially thought to be the sole source of. Different types of relationships can lead people to develop a dependency behavior.

Love Story with an Addict

A person who they love, to plunge into the depths of addiction could be detrimental for people. If they learn of the addict in their relationship emotions of despair and jealousy could be felt by the spouse of an addict . This can lead to a rise in codependency within the relationship. Everyone would like to assist those they love when they're struggling. However, codependent spouses of addicts may not be aware the fact that their dependency is fueling the addiction's behaviour. They may not realize that their spouse comes home later, doesn't want to talk about their day in a way that is too loud or spends more family's money than they did previously, or engages in other unsavory behaviors. They think that their partner might have been cheating, they are annoyed and jealous. As they were thinking they were having some sort of affair with them, they find out that it's more serious than that, addiction.

A romantic relationship with an abusive

Codependency is a common trait among people who grow up, but it is it is also normal for people to be codependent later on in life. A relationship that is abusive can tear an individual until they are unable to recognize themselves. Someone who is confident and strong may be able to spot red flags and flee the scene at the first indication of abuse. If a person is deficient in self-esteem, they may be more vulnerable to the possibility of becoming dependent in an abusive relationship, and may not ever.

Growing up with a resentful Parent

The majority of parents do their best in raising their children. There are times when you hear parents give the old-fashioned address about the way they feed their children they changed them, made sure they were safe to keep them safe, offered them food and placed the child's needs ahead of their own. Most of the time they are true but they aren't anything to boast about. Parents are expected to perform the things they are supposed to do. If you decide to introduce an innocent child into the world, expecting your child to take care of themselves, feed or even provide for themself is a pity. Though most parents realize this, and use only the traditional phrase when they're disappointed with their children, some parents have grudges with their children or feel resentful towards them.

Growing up with a Narcissist

If a self-centered emotional underdeveloped and young person has a child and they are able to develop codependency because of feeling that they are not important. Self-centered parents place their own priorities first and show their children that seeking things for themselves is a sign of greed. The idea that self-care is a form of greed can put a child at risk of developing a dependency. Children learn that they need to place their parents' desires and needs before their own in order to become a better person. Narcissists think that their own opinions are the only thing that is important, which causes the child to feel invisible and unappreciated.

Growing up with an Addict

Family-based addiction is among the main reasons why kids develop codependency. Parents who are addicted can create numerous problems for their children's lives both in the past and into the future when their children grow up. Children of addicts can develop a fear of confronting their parents because they will be extremely angry if faced with questions. They are not able to have confidence in anyone, and they are blamed for other errors since they were forced to hide their parents' addiction from others and learnt that if have a relationship with someone, it is best to will keep their secrets, even if it hurts them.

Different types of codependents

One kind of codependent could seek to earn their partner's respect, love and love more actively While another kind could be more inactive. When both people who codepend on each other stop in their quest to win the trust of their partners they may experience the third kind of codependency, anorexia.

• Passive codependency Codependents who are passive fear conflict, and try to stay clear of it. Low self-esteem and low self-esteem in the passive codependent person create an extremely high risk of attracting dangerous or abusive individuals.

• Active Codependency Codependents who are active often are mistaken for narcissists due to their obvious methods of manipulating and control their companions. They're not like passive codependents and neither do they have a fear of conflicts. They are awed by an argument , because they see it as a means of getting to confront their partner with their inability to reciprocate.

* Codependency Anorexia occurs when codependents realize that there's no way to win at the conclusion of their exhausting struggle with their uncaring partner they may be willing to give up all their behavior patterns. It doesn't mean they end their dependency. It is merely turning their emotions off to avoid being able to fall prey to the traps of abusers and narcissists.

Anorexia caused by codependency is the final option for someone who does not manage their problems. The realization that those they thought were the perfect match always ended up becoming the one who hurt' renders codependents ineffective. Instead of looking in the mirror at themselves and recognizing that they're at the root of the problem they fear that each person they meet could cause harm to them.

When Codependency Endes

If you're dependent on one person, or are dependent on a destructive habit, you might think that you are unable to begin something unless the person or the habit is always present. It can be difficult to believe that everything is difficult without them . It isn't a matter of trying something new or not, you feel that you are unable to move away from them or without them.

In the absence of your dependence, you might feel depressed and feel like you are unable to exert a bit of effort in your direction to get through your day. It's like you were in a state of paralysis, not having a clear vision, or being able to decide how to proceed and.

You suddenly feel exhausted from your day-to-day activities You are not able to tolerate the people who surround you. Everything you once enjoyed is now a hassle and you are emotionally overwhelmed sometimes. It could be that you're going through a myriad of emotional shifts which make it impossible for you to live your normal life. Your mind can't stop being in constant debate with itself. Codependency could be a sign that you're too attached to your partner and do not like or know how to be with you and with yourself although you might be in a relationship.

So, how do you end all the dependence habits that are preventing you from moving forward living your life? How do you get away from being totally and unhealthy dependent on someone else? Furthermore do you need to do to regain your self-worth?

But, what are the habits you like to eliminate?

* It could be that you are prone to not feel loved by your spouse.

A different habit is to fear your partner going away.

* You made jealousy a habit.

* Your partner's opinion is more important than your own This is a different routine.

* You're a fan of demanding your partner's attention even when you think it's unreasonable. Guess what? This is another way of life.

You know the ways you're reacting and acting, yet you think you are unable to change as your genes were shaped by these patterns.

You make it appear that things are good because they are your routine.

* You've become an extremely frustrated person who can't be any more with their partner.

Change Your Mental State

To fully benefit from your inherent abilities and traits You must also make your brain perform the tasks you would like it to perform for you, exactly like an exerciser you're working out.

If you are looking to break free from codependency the person with whom you share an intimate relationship with, then you have to educate your brain (and all of you) to either end your dependence on them or become completely independent.

What can you do to accomplish this? What can you do to workout an area of your body that is difficult to reach? It's not really impossible to reach your brain since every time you think, speak or even communicate you're already making use of your brain. If you wish to break the cycle of dependency and become independent, you have to educate your brain to think differently.

Be in a state of mind where mindfulness is habit and you are at ease enough to ask yourself questions that you are uncomfortable asking. The state of mindfulness is one mind that lets you be aware of many of problems, if you are willing to let it happen naturally. The great thing about it is that it's totally free, as you can't make anyone else help you with it.

You must be willing to make a change

We're doing things in similar to how we aren't even unsure of the things we do. We're also accustomed to feeling certain emotions so strongly that it's best to maintain them like this, so that we don't become lost in our identity when those feelings cease to exist. It's a terribly important fact that requires you to be flexible and to be active as if you are uncomfortable, to inquire and to be doubtful of your own self when needed. A second fact is that if you're unwilling to step out of the way and discover new things, you'll do exactly the same thing and achieve the same results.

This type of codependency can be able to disappear if you begin to establish and nurture yourself. Your relationship with yourself is the most significant one.

Take a Break every now and then

It's fine to request some time off and recharge batteries. No one should ever try to convince you otherwise.

You can request a break if you think breaking up with your partner isn't something you'd like to do your heart. One option is to take a break in this manner, if both parties agree, you can start rebuilding your relationship and then see whether it still is a spark that can keep the flame or is near to ending.

Breaks can also indicate that you're spending time with someone else. This means you are able to see more clearly what is the reason you are dependent on one another. A break can lead you to view things from a different perspective energy, perspective, and motivation.

Establish Some Boundaries

Did you consider that a codependency issue might be that you do not set boundaries because you're afraid of what your partner could do or think of that they might not like the limits that you've set? Setting limits is something that we must all be doing, particularly when you're the kind of person who will sacrifice your own needs to meet the needs of someone else. There's a line that all share that we must not overstep it.

A personal boundary can help you when you are unsure about something and you begin to think about pleasing another person instead of pleasing yourself. When you set limits and boundaries, you'll also be able to remain loyal to yourself since nobody else is accountable for the way you conduct yourself. If someone else let you violate your invisible boundary and you weren't happy with it, well you made the right choice by letting them in.

Limits don't mean that you can tell your partner "no" as a solution. There are a lot more limitations you could discuss together with your spouse. Examples:

* There are boundaries for sexuality especially in recent times as there is an increase in open relationships polyamorous and polygamous relationships.

There are some boundaries to communication which may range from the way you refer to each other (as as in your name for one another) or the words you do not want to say about each other.

There are boundaries in space. If you don't live together , but you are spending excessive time at one another's homes. Perhaps you're living in a relationship, but want to keep your own identity.

There are boundaries in the economy that allow you to share your money, in which you share a portion of it, divide your earnings or you don't share your wealth.

There are boundaries to commitment. These are typically more prevalent when couples begin to know each other.

If your partner makes you feel guilty for not having a clear line because you have set your boundaries that you have set, then you need to have an honest conversation with them. It's not an argument that demands one to win and one to lose. This is, however, an argument that requires two adults with the ability to debate their boundaries with a conscious mind.

Find a New Activity or Find a new hobby

A new pastime or interest could be a wonderful method to break away from the old habits and patterns that we've become accustomed to. This can also mean that you have to step outside from your normal routine in order to be a part of the experience.

If you're in a relationship that is codependent, it is likely that you be hearing your partner say "don't make it happen" and you'll not even think about it even though it has been your dream. However, if you're the one who tells your partner to not go and you're ruining dreams of someone else because it's not yours.

How Codependency Functions

Do not ask people to pay for their own expense

Dependents are people-pleasers. That is, they do their best to meet the desires and needs of all those who surrounds them. They're always the first to answer calls for assistance. They are the "hero" chromosome within them always makes them the front of the line of rescuers and aiders when they're required. They have a strong desire to assist and they feed on the issues of their relatives and friends members. Ofttimes, they offer help and assistance at the expense of themselves. They will go to the extreme even in the event of burning in order to become indispensable to anyone who might need assistance.

Feeling uncomfortable when receiving attention or the support of others

Codependents, unfortunately, not have a problem seeking and receiving help. They're taught to keep their feelings and desires in the back of their minds throughout their development and are unable to allow themselves to reveal what they perceive as an weakness. So, they live in silence. They do not seek assistance and prefer to navigate the water by themselves. If they get help, like cash donations or an unaffordable recommendation, they become overwhelmed and confused on how to respond. This is why they stay in situations where others do not even realize they need assistance. They can also hide their absence of a visible perception of having a lot. Even with the same partner they're dependent and are unable to separate anything from the feeling of appreciation.

Look at themselves through the eyes of Other People

Codependents are among the most self-critical people in the world. They lack self-confidence, which makes them feel anxious and unsure of the opinions of others and their perceptions of their lives. In this way, they could present a false image to attract attention, but remain mostly empty inside. They aren't able to handle negative criticism and can be aggressive or take the extra step to avoid criticism altogether. In the end, for them however, they are enthralled by how their spouse views their partner. Does he consider them absolutely essential? Do they represent the sole port of call in case he falls into trouble? These are the crucial questions that occupy the minds of codependents.

You can conveniently ignore Red Flags

Particularly in their relationships, people who are codependent do not detect the indications. Inspiring because of their dependence upon their partner and a fear of rocking their boat, or to avoid conflicts. They shy away from solving problems in their relationships until it's too late. They continue to ignore warning signs and do not listen to warnings and obvious clues.

Reframe the mistakes made by others

This is what causes codependency at the end of the day. There is always a an excuse that they can use to justify what their partner's behavior is not in line with social norms. Alcoholism? He had troubled childhood. Are you addicted to gambling? He doesn't play as often. In addition, he's rich. Their arsenal of excuses never runs out. Even when a partner realizes that there is a problem that requires a solution the partner will instead insist that they're there, rather than work together in finding a solution.

Don't Give Less Than What They Get in relationships

It is a constant feature of friendships that one partner is more attentive or attention over the others. Codependent individuals constantly suppress the voice of their own demands. They are not demanding any amount, if anything, and are afraid to express their thoughts. So, it's not surprising to find them often giving away more than they get. However, the majority times they be suffering from "bigger issues" which demand their attention rather than taking note on the amount of attention they get.

Say Yes, Everytime

A codependent is not aware or say "NO" in response to any demand. He is never hesitant about offering a service if you can, no matter how far he will go to offer it. However, this doesn't mean that you are able to handle any task, but. The only thing he has done is to make himself uncomfortable before the thought of disappointing other person. In the context of an early life that was likely looking for the approval and approval of parents who were difficult and perhaps uncompromising siblings, it's simple to see why notion of not accepting the request could be unfamiliar to someone who is codependent.

Feelings of guilt or responsibility for the suffering of others

The initial stage of codependency results from an increased sense of responsibility and obligation to assist others in overcoming their struggles. Particularly for those who have become dependent due to being required to meet the needs of an unwell relative or friend and are engulfed by the notion of being the sole person with the ability to aid every person in their life. They feel a sense of guilt when they are not able to stop the flow of suffering that a friend is suffering. They view it as an act of failure when they aren't considered as helping to ease suffering, or when their efforts don't yield outcomes. They lower their standards and limit their efforts to accommodate the needs of others. Their love for others is what brings them joy and happiness When people are hurt this, it creates a feeling of guilt.

Reluctance to share your thoughts or feelings of fear of offending others

Children who develop to be dependent learn not to express emotions or confess weaknesses. They are able to become adults but not capable of intimacy. In this case, the word "intimacy is not a reference to sexual intimacy, even though it is also believed that it is affected. In this case, it is the capacity to express their emotions, feelings, and needs with their partner and to be able to assert equality as partners. In fear of offending others or fearing they might offend those who ask for assistance They keep their real feelings in themselves and give it with the crowd.

How does codependency affect conflict couples?

Codependency continues to perpetuate due to different reasons. If you're a codependent individual you should take the time to learn the causes of codependency, so that you can seek ways to conquer these. You are your own enemy and that's the reason you have to fight codependency. Self-defeating is a regular issue if you aren't worthy of the best life. Sure, you may have made a few mistakes in the past. However, not allowing yourself to forgive yourself for past mistakes isn't the right choice. You begin to deny your strengths and thinking.

After you have recognized codependency you'll be unable to conquer it due to self-sabotage that can make you feel less than worthy. To deal with codependency, it is important that you need to be convinced that you are worthy. Consider how someone who is self-loved would take care of the situation you are currently in. Self-loved people is not likely to make decisions which could hurt their body and mind.

If you aren't sure that you love yourself, try to fool yourself for a few days and you'll eventually become real. Self-sabotage is closing the perception, and this is the reason you're struggling to perceive the reality. If you attempt to make it appear real, you'll be able get the job done in a slow, steady manner. When you look at factors like anger, denial, or shame, they can perpetuate codependency in a matter of minutes. Learn about the causes to help you overcome them.

It is important to acknowledge the existence of dependence as it could be risky. If you are denying it, then it is a sign that you're not ready to embrace change and accept it so it will persist. Instead of confronting the challenges that you face you are more determined to shield others from their own problems. This same pattern repeats in the event that you refuse to acknowledge that you're dependent.

Refuse to deny your partner's behavior

The idea of denying your partner's actions is among the most common lies, but there is a way to over come it. You are unable to admit the fact that you partner may be addicted , and the addiction of your partner causes many issues within your life. But, you're not willing to accept it and that is the reason why codependency persists in your life. This type of denial is typical because codependents have faced similar situations since their childhood. They may have grew up with parents who have addiction issues and it appears like normal behavior to them.

Dependents and addicts are used to being treated as if they were their own, which is why they're not yet ready to assume on the burden. They are also comfortable with this because they prefer taking care of other people.

If you are unable to accept the actions of your partner it is important to recognize that you're headed toward a dangerous path. You have to accept the facts and take action accordingly, because relationships can destroy your life if it isn't handled manage it properly. You have to recognize that you're not accountable for their behavior. If they are dependent or dependent on you for nearly everything, then that you are the one who has created the conditions to it. Don't let anyone harm you simply because you're dependent. If you don't acknowledge the actions of your partner isn't a sign that you aren't concerned about their actions. Of course, you're worried, but you do not see the severity or come up with arguments to justify the behavior. This is the normal behavior of someone who is in love with their spouse, but codependents who love each other show more. They don't bother to rectify their mistakes, they simply leave them alone. In reality, ignorance can cause more harm.

Refusal to acknowledge codependency

If you're confronted by codependency, it is likely that you'll dismiss it. This is the first step. It is evident you're a codependent but you're not ready to accept it since you think that it's the result of a situation which has led you to become codependent. You attempt to put the blame on the circumstance or other people to avoid having to need to talk about codependency. The majority of codependents do not want to think about it , because they fear that it will make their pain worse however it won't.

Another reason is that you're the type of person who needs support from others. If you recognize that you're dependent, you'll need seek assistance from others to manage the problem. This kind of thinking can lead you down a destructive path. It's not your favorite that someone else is caring for you and taking responsibility for your behavior because for a long time you've done it for other people. You don't want people to be happy, as this can trigger self-reflection at some time. If you're codependent, it is easy to avoid self-examination. This is the reason you refused assistance from other people.

The act of denying your true nature, that is codependency, will aid you in staying far from seeking help from professionals and to admit your dependence. However certain codependents do not seek out professional assistance, but they seek to handle them all on their own. They believe they can solve the issue through talking to their close family members and by reading reliable articles and books. Sometimes, this could be risky depending on the degree of dependence that you experience. It is possible that you are embarrassed to seek help, which is why you avoid getting to experts. However, keep in mind that it's not a good idea.

Conclusion

The workplace can be a relaxing environment; however, it could also be a source that causes stress. I would like to think that you have learned some suggestions and strategies for handling any conflicts that might be arising. But, these suggestions can easily be referenced for avoiding the situation completely. As previously mentioned, the concepts are able to be applied in your personal life as well.